Retirement Systems in Japan

Books published by the
PENSION RESEARCH COUNCIL:

Actuarial Aspects of Pension Security—*William F. Marples (1964)*
A New Look at Accounting for Pension Costs—*William D. Hall & David L. Landsittel (1979)*
Collectively Bargained Multi-Employer Pension Plans—*Joseph J. Melone (1963)*
Concepts of Actuarial Soundness in Pension Plans—*Dorrance C. Bronson (1957)*
Continuing Care Retirement Communities—*Howard E. Winklevoss & Alwyn Powell (1985)*
Decision and Influence Process in Private Pension Plans—*James E. McNulty, Jr. (1961)*
Economics of Pension Insurance—*Richard A. Ippolito (1989)*
Employer Accounting for Pensions—*Ernest L. Hicks & C. L. Trowbridge (1985)*
Employer Guarantee of Pension Benefits—*Dan M. McGill (1970)*
Ensuring Medical Care for the Aged—*Mortimer Spiegelman (1960)*
Financing the Civil Service Retirement System—*Dan M. McGill, ed. (1979)*
Fulfilling Pension Expectations—*Dan M. McGill (1962)*
Fundamentals of Private Pensions—*Dan M. McGill (1955, 1964, 1975, 1979, and 1984 editions)*
Fundamentals of Private Pensions—*Dan M. McGill and Donald S. Grubbs, 6th edition (1989)*
Guaranty Fund for Private Pension Obligations—*Dan M. McGill (1970)*
Indexation of Pension and Other Benefits—*Robert J. Myers (1978)*
Inflataion and Pensions—*Susan M. Watcher (1988)*
It's My Retirement Money—Take Good Care of It: The TIAA-CREF Story—*William C. Greenough (1990)*
Joint Trust Pension Plans—*Daniel F. McGinn (1979)*
Legal Protection of Private Pension Expectations—*Edwin W. Patterson (1960)*
Legal Status of Employee Benefit Rights under Private Pension Plans—*Benjamin Aaron (1961)*
Pension Asset Management—*Leslie Hannah (1988)*
Pension Mathematics—*Howard Winklevoss (1977)*
Pension Tax Policy in the United States—*Richard A. Ippolito (1990)*
Pensions, Economics and Public Policy—*Richard A. Ippolito (1985)*
Positive Experiences in Retirement—*Otto Pollak (1957)*
Preservation of Pension Benefit Rights—*Dan M. McGill (1972)*
Proxy Voting of Pension Plan Equity Securities—*Dan M. McGill, ed. (1989)*
Reciprocity among Private Multi-Employer Pension Plans—*Maurice E. McDonald (1975)*
Retirement Systems for Public Employees—*Thomas Bleakney (1973)*
Search for a National Retirement Income Policy—*Jack L. Van Derhei, ed. (1987)*
Social Aspects of Retirement—*Otto Pollak (1956)*
Social Investing—*Dan M. McGill, ed. (1984)*
Social Security and Private Pension Plans—*Dan M. McGill, ed. (1977)*
Status of Funding under Private Pension Plans—*Frank L. Griffin, Jr. & Charles L. Trowbridge (1969)*

Retirement Systems in Japan

Robert L. Clark
Department of Economics and Business
North Carolina State University

Ralph H. Blanchard Memorial Endowment Series
Volume IV

Published for the
Pension Research Council
Wharton School
University of Pennsylvania
by

IRWIN

Homewood, IL 60430
Boston, MA 02116

Sponsoring editor: Michael W. Junior
Project editor: Paula M. Buschman
Production manager: Diane Palmer
Compositor: BookMasters, Inc.
Typeface: 11/13 Melior
Printer: Arcata Graphics/Kingsport

Library of Congress Cataloging-in-Publication Data

Clark, Robert Louis.
    Retirement systems in Japan / Robert L. Clark.
        p.   cm. — (Ralph H. Blanchard memorial endowment series ; v. 4)
     ISBN 0–256–09141–2
     1. Old age pensions—Japan.   2. Retirement income—Japan.
   3. Social security—Japan. I. Title. II. Series.
   HD7105.35.J3C56 1991
   331.25'2'0952—dc20   90–4531
                                                     CIP

Printed in the United States of America
1 2 3 4 5 6 7 8 9 0   K   7 6 5 4 3 2 1 0

PENSION RESEARCH COUNCIL

PURPOSE OF THE COUNCIL

Founded in 1952, the Pension Research Council is one of several research organizations within the Wharton School of the University of Pennsylvania. As part of the nation's first school of business, the Council functions in a bracing environment of academic freedom and objectivity. The basic purpose of the Council is to undertake research that will have the effect of strengthening those arrangements designed to provide the financial resources needed for a secure and dignified old age. It seeks to broaden public understanding of these complex arrangements through basic research into their social, economic, legal, actuarial, and financial foundations. Although geared to the long view of the pension institution, projects undertaken by the Council are always relevant to real world concerns and frequently focus on issues under current debate.

The Council is composed of individuals from large corporate plan sponsors, organized labor, actuarial consulting firms, the accounting profession, the legal profession, investment counselors, banks, insurance companies, not-for-profit organizations, and several academic disciplines. The Council does not speak with one voice and espouses no particular point of view. The members do share a general desire to encourage and strengthen private-sector approaches to old age economic security, while recognizing the essential role of social security and other income maintenance programs in the public sector.

The members of the Council are appointed by the Dean of the Wharton School and serve indeterminate terms. The Council reviews the findings of current research projects, acts to generate new research proposals, and reviews external proposals. In performing these functions, the members identify areas in which additional research is needed, consider the general form the research should take, then evaluate the qualifications of persons deemed capable of carrying out the approved projects.

The research projects are carried out by persons commissioned under individually designed ad hoc arrangements. The researchers are normally academic scholars, but nonacademic experts with special qualifications for the tasks involved may be used. The research findings are reviewed by members of the Council, who may offer criticism as to both the substance of the report and the inferences drawn from the studies. The author of any manuscript is free to accept or reject the criticisms of the Council members, but the latter have the privilege of recording in the published document their dissent from any interpretative statements or points of view expressed by the author. Whether or not written dissents are included, publication should not be interpreted to indicate either agreement or disagreement by the Council or its individual members with the substance of the document or its inferences.

ACKNOWLEDGMENTS

My interest in Japanese retirement policies developed during a series of visits to Japan in 1988–89. On these occasions, I was a visiting researcher at Nihon University Population Research Institute in Tokyo. The staff of NUPRI was very generous in providing research resources and helping locate numerous pension experts in Japan. I wish to thank Hideo Ibe, Japan Foundation for Research and Development of Pension Schemes; Eiji Mizutani and David Crawford, The Wyatt Co.–Tokyo; Kiyoshi Owada, president of Pension Fund Association; Junichi Sakamoto, deputy director, Actuarial Affairs Division, Pension Bureau, Ministry of Health and Welfare; Toshio Suzuki, Japan Federation of Employers' Association; and Noriyasu Watanabe, Research Institute of Life Insurance Welfare, for taking time to discuss the Japanese pension system with me. Kiyoshi Murakami, Nippon Dantai Life Insurance Company, provided several of his papers and other pension information. A special thanks goes to Naohiro Ogawa, NUPRI, who made my trips to Japan possible and taught me about the economic and demographic conditions of Japan. Toru Nakaya provided valuable translation assistance. Richard Ippolito has made many valuable comments on several drafts of this manuscript.

CONTENTS

List of Tables and Figures   xiii

1 **Introduction**   1
   Overview of Retirement Programs   1
   Population Aging in Japan   4
   Implications of Population Aging   7
   Framework for Analysis   10

2 **Work and Retirement**   12
   Labor Markets and Employment Contracts   12
   Mandatory Retirement   14
   Work after Retirement   17
   Government Employment Policies   19
   Labor Force Participation Rates   21
   Retirement Policies in an Aging Society   23

3 **Social Security Retirement Benefit Systems**   27
   Increasing Costs and the Need for Reform   30
   National Pension   34
   Employees' Pension Insurance   38
   Social Security: Problems and Prospects   46

4 **Tax Policy, Private Retirement Plans, and**
   Lump-Sum Payments   52
   Tax Policy and Retirement Income   52
   Coverage by Retirement Plans   59
   Lump-Sum Severance Pay   60
   Changing Nature of Lump-Sum Plans   65

5 **Private Pension Plans**   69
   Tax-Qualified Pensions   70

Employees' Pension Funds 74
Nonqualified Private Pensions 84
Comparing Employees' Pension Funds and
    Tax-Qualified Pensions 85

**6 Lessons from the Japanese Experience
for U.S. Pension Policy** 94

LIST OF TABLES AND FIGURES

Tables

1.1. Population Ratios: Japan and United States   6
1.2. Projection of Pension Expenditures:
     Developed Countries   10
2.1. Proportion of Employees Who Are Part-Time
     Workers by Firm Size   13
2.2. Distribution of Mandatory Retirement Ages   17
2.3. Mandatory Retirement Age and Size of Firm   17
2.4. Average Retirement Age by Industry   18
2.5. Labor Force Participation Rates of Men Aged 65
     and Older   18
2.6. Age-Specific Labor Force Participation Rates   21
3.1. Statutory Pension Schemes   29
3.2. Employees' Pension Insurance Contribution Rates   30
3.3. Trends and Projections of Participants, Beneficiaries,
     and Contribution Rates: Employees' Pension
     Insurance   31
3.4. National Pension Contribution Amounts   32
3.5. Trends and Projections of Participants, Beneficiaries,
     and Contribution Amounts: National Pension   32
3.6. Social Security Trust Fund Reserves   33
3.7. Early Retirement Penalties and Delayed Retirement
     Credits for National Pension   37
3.8. Insurable Period for National Pension   38
3.9. Schedule of Monthly Insured Remuneration for
     Employees' Pension Insurance System   40
3.10. Coefficients and Unit Amounts Under Transitional
     Provisions of Employees' Pension Insurance
     Scheme   41
4.1. Coverage By Retirement Benefit Plans   59

4.2.	Voluntary Retirement Benefits as Percent of Involuntary Retirement Benefits	61
4.3.	Minimum Service Requirements for Eligibility for Lump-Sum Severance Payment	62
4.4.	Lump-Sum Retirement Allowance for Involuntary Termination	63
5.1.	Number of Tax-Qualified Pension Plans	73
5.2.	Tax-Qualified Pension Funds Invested in Insurance Companies and Trust Banks	74
5.3.	Size Distribution of Employees' Pension Funds	75
5.4.	Industrial Distribution of Employees' Pension Funds	76
5.5.	Terminations and Mergers in Employees' Pension Funds	82
5.6.	Contributions to Pension Guaranty System	84
5.7.	Participants in Employees' Pension Funds and Tax-Qualified Plans	86
5.8.	Pension Coverage among Firms Listed on Japanese Stock Exchange	87
5.9.	Number of Beneficiaries and Average Benefit Amounts	88
5.10.	Pension Fund Assets Managed by Trust Banks	90
5.11.	Total Assets Managed by Insurance Companies	91

Figures

1.1.	Coverage by Retirement Income Plans	3
1.2.	Ratio of Persons 65 and Older to Total Population	7
1.3.	Birth and Death Rates in Japan	8
1.4.	Trend in Life Expectancy at Birth	9
3.1.	Change in Total Social Security Benefits Due to 1985 Pension Reform: Average Married Retired Employee	43
5.1.	Amount of Guaranteed Pension Payment to Terminated Employees' Pension Funds	83

CHAPTER 1

Introduction

The Japanese system of retirement programs consists of a network of public and private income plans for older persons. These programs include a two-part social security system, the traditional payment of a lump-sum severance benefit by the company to retiring workers, and the recently established system of private pension plans. Retirement decisions are made within the framework of company personnel policies requiring retirement at designated ages. Public and private retirement policies in Japan have evolved during the past 50 years as the economy developed and the population aged. This report examines current retirement policies in Japan and contrasts them to similar policies in the United States. By understanding these Japanese programs and their implications, we will be better able to respond to problems arising in U.S. retirement policies.

OVERVIEW OF RETIREMENT PROGRAMS

Along with the United States, Japan introduced its social security program in the middle of the 20th century, much later than other developed countries did. The initial social security program in Japan was established in the 1940s and covered only certain types of employees. Over time, a series of public pension schemes were developed to cover other categories of workers. By 1960, most workers were covered by one of these government retirement programs. The largest of these social security programs were Employees' Pension Insurance, covering most employees in the private sector, and the National Pension Plan, covering self-employed workers.

1

As these social security programs matured and the population aged, expenditures on retirement programs rose rapidly. In 1985, the social security system was substantially modified. Prior to 1985, the National Pension Plan covered only self-employed workers and, on a voluntary basis, their spouses. The 1985 amendments restructured the National Pension Plan into a universal plan providing a flat benefit per year of credited service for all persons. The Employees' Pension Insurance program now provides an earnings-related benefit to covered employees. Thus, self-employed workers are covered only by the National Pension Plan, while employees are covered by the National Pension Plan and the Employees' Pension Insurance program.

In addition to social security, most retiring workers receive some form of retirement payment from their employers. Historically, most firms gave workers a lump-sum payment at retirement. In the 1960s, legislation was enacted that excluded employer contributions to pension plans paying retirement annuities from being taxed as current income to employees. Tax-qualified pension plans were introduced in 1962. These plans may be established by firms with as few as 15 workers. Although they offer a pension annuity, most plans have a lump-sum option, and most retirees select this option.

In 1966, legislation was enacted that permitted firms to adopt employees' pension funds. Companies that institute employees' pension funds assume the responsibility for payment of the earnings-related component of social security (the Employees' Pension Insurance benefit) and provide an added benefit equal to at least 30 percent of this "contracted out" part of social security. Over half of the employees covered by the Employees' Pension Insurance component of the social security system are participants in either a tax-qualified pension or an employees' pension fund. Since the 1960s, pensions have spread throughout the economy, especially among large firms, and pensions are beginning to replace lump-sum payment plans as the primary form of retirement benefit.

An outline of coverage by retirement plans in Japan is shown in Figure 1–1. All public workers are covered by either a statutory plan covering national public workers or a plan covering local public workers. In the private sector, all workers are covered by the National Pension Plan. For self-employed workers, this is the only form of retirement plan except for individual savings. In addition to the National Pension Plan, employees are covered by one of three statutory pension plans. Most employees are covered by the Employees' Pension Insurance program.

On top of these statutory plans, most private employees are also covered by private pensions, either tax-qualified plans or employees'

FIGURE 1–1 Coverage by Retirement Income Plans

	Private-Sector Workers		Public-Sector Workers
	Employees	*Self-Employed*	
Statutory pension schemes: Mandatory coverage	National Pension plus earnings-related plan 1. Employees' Pension Insurance 2. Private school teachers and employees' M.A.A. or 3. Agricultural, forestry and fishery institutions employees' M.A.A.	National Pension	National Pension plus earnings-related plan 1. National public service M.A.A. or 2. Local public service M.A.A.
Private retirement income plan	Virtually all firms offer either 1. Lump-sum severance plan 2. Tax-qualified pension plan 3. Employees' pension fund 4. Lump-sum plan plus one of the two types of pensions		Most public workers are covered by a lump-sum severance plan

Note: M.A.A. indicates Mutual Aid Association.

pension funds, or a lump-sum severance payment plan. A married retired employee who had earned the average wage will receive a total social security benefit equal to 69 percent of his final earnings, excluding bonuses. If covered by an employees' pension fund paying the minimum required supplemental benefit, this replacement rate increases to 78 percent. Self-employed workers will have a much lower retirement benefit unless they have engaged in substantial savings during their work life.

The Japanese system of industrial relations is characterized by long-term employment for regular workers coupled with mandatory retirement at a relatively young age. Earnings tend to rise with seniority, and retirement benefits are based on final pay. Retirees are often rehired but at lower wages and with the loss of seniority rights. Despite these policies, the labor force participation rates of older Japanese are the highest in the developed world.

As the population and the labor force have aged, the Japanese labor market has adjusted to the rising cost of retirement programs and the increased labor costs associated with an older work force. The close linkage among compensation, firm retirement policies, and pensions requires an understanding of each prior to an assessment of retirement systems in Japan. The primary objective of this study is to examine the retirement programs and policies in Japan and to determine how they are changing in response to an aging population.

The remainder of this chapter provides the framework for our analysis by examining the recent aging of the Japanese population and assessing the response of retirement programs to population aging. The next chapter examines the Japanese system of industrial relations and how it affects the labor force participation of older persons. Chapter 2 also reviews recent government employment policies for older workers. Subsequent chapters examine the social security system and the system of private retirement benefit programs. Throughout the analysis, the evolution of these programs is reviewed, and their responsiveness to population aging is highlighted. Specific attention is paid to differences between the Japanese retirement system and that prevailing in the United States.

POPULATION AGING IN JAPAN

Throughout the course of world economic development, the real incomes and living standards of nations have increased. In response to these conditions, birthrates have fallen, health conditions have improved, and life expectancy has risen. These changes have produced an aging of populations in most countries. Work rates of older workers tend to decline with economic development.[1] The typical pattern of development is for countries to experience aging populations along with declines in the work rates of older persons. These changes increase the ratio of retired older persons to active workers, thus increasing the cost of public and private retirement plans.

In the second half of the 20th century, all developed countries have faced the economic and political problems of providing for their aging populations. National retirement systems have been instituted in most countries, and the costs of these programs have risen sharply. The projected continued population aging will further increase the cost of public and private retirement programs.

The Japanese experience is similar to that of the other developed countries, except its population aging and the development of retirement programs have occurred later than in the other developed countries. However, the Japanese population is now rapidly aging. The public and private pension systems instituted after 1940 are now attempting to adjust to this changing demographic environment.

Japan is one of the most rapidly aging countries in the world.[2] Table 1–1 shows that the proportion of the population age 65 and over rose from 4.9 percent in 1950 to 9.1 percent in 1980. By 1990, the proportion of the population age 65 and over is expected to be 11.9 percent. It is projected to increase to 20.5 percent in 2010 before rising to almost 25 percent by 2020. Figure 1–2 compares the increase in the proportion of the population age 65 and over in Japan to several other developed countries. The figure indicates that in the 1950s, the elderly population in Japan was a much smaller proportion of the total population than it was in the other developed countries. The rapid aging of the Japanese population is expected to produce one of the oldest populations in the world within the next 20 years.

This aging of the population occurred in response to sharp declines in the birthrate following a postwar baby boom. Figure 1–3 indicates a relatively stable birthrate over the first third of the 20th century, followed by a gradual decline until World War II. During the war, birthrates dropped sharply. After the end of World War II, Japan experienced a postwar baby boom, as did most other countries. However, in Japan this boom lasted for only three years, from 1947 to 1949, before birthrates again began to fall. By contrast, birthrates in the United States remained relatively high until the early 1960s.

Accompanying the decline in births has been a rapid decline in death rates. Reduced mortality has substantially increased life expectancy in Japan (see Figure 1–4). At present, life expectancy at birth in Japan is among the highest for any nation.[3] In 1987, life expectancy at birth for women was 82.1 years and for men was 75.9 years. This means life expectancy has increased by 33 years for women and 29 years for men since 1935. This rapid aging of the Japanese population since 1950 is contrasted in Table 1–1 to the more gradual aging of the U.S. population. Between 1950 and 2020, the proportion of the population age 65 and over is expected to increase by fivefold in Japan but only double in the U.S.

The rapid pace of population aging in Japan is illustrated by comparing the time it will take for the population age 65 and over to increase from 7 percent to 14 percent of the total population to the time required for similar demographic changes in other developed countries. In Japan, this doubling of the older population will require only 25 years and is expected to occur between 1970 and 1995. By contrast, similar population aging required 45 years in the United Kingdom and West Germany (1930–1975); in the United States, it will take 70 years to occur (1945–2015). In France, this doubling of the proportion of the population age 65 and older evolved over 115 years (1865–1980).[4]

TABLE 1–1 Population Ratios: Japan and United States

	Japan			United States		
Year	Age 65 and over / Total population	Age 65 and over / Ages 20–64	Ages 20–24 / Ages 20–64	Age 65 and over / Total population	Age 65 and over / Ages 20–64	Ages 20–24 / Ages 20–64
1950	4.9%	10.0%	18.8%	8.1%	14.1%	13.2%
1960	5.7	10.6	16.4	9.2	17.7	11.8
1970	7.1	11.7	17.0	9.8	18.7	16.0
1980	9.1	15.1	11.1	11.3	19.8	16.7
1990	11.9	19.4	11.8	12.6	21.4	12.7
2000	16.3	26.7	10.8	13.0	21.8	11.0
2010	20.5	35.7	9.0	13.9	22.8	11.3
2020	24.6	44.8	10.9	17.7	30.2	10.4

SOURCE: Japanese data were provided by Naohiro Ogawa, Nihon University Population Research Institute. Data for 1950 to 1980 are derived from the Japanese Census. Data for 1990 to 2020 are based on Ogawa's projections. U.S. data are from U.S. Bureau of Census, "Projections of Population of the United States by Age, Sex, and Race: 1988 to 2080," *Current Population Reports*, Series P-25, no. 1018 (Washington, D.C.: U.S. Government Printing Office, 1989). Projections are from the middle series.

FIGURE 1–2 Ratio of Persons Age 65 and Older to Total Population, Various Countries

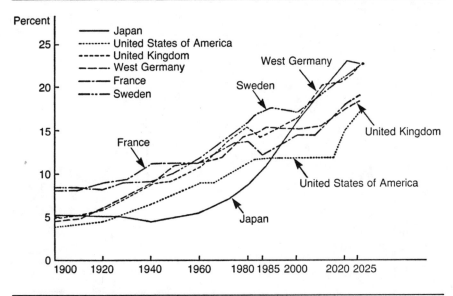

SOURCE: Social Insurance Agency, *Outline of Social Insurance in Japan,* 1988, p. 9.

Postwar fertility patterns have had a dramatic effect on the age structure of the labor force. During the early 1970s, a large number of young workers entered the labor force. Fertility declines after 1950 resulted in a sharp drop in the number of persons entering the labor force after 1975. This is reflected in the decline in the ratio of persons age 20 to 24 to persons age 20 to 64 from 17 percent in 1970 to an estimated 11.8 percent in 1990 (see Table 1–1). As a result, the average age of the labor force increased, and the number of older workers increased rapidly. The average age of employed persons rose slightly from 31 years in 1962 to 33.1 years in 1970. However, by 1988 the mean age of workers had increased to 38 years.[5]

IMPLICATIONS OF POPULATION AGING

The aging of the population and the labor force has confronted Japan with a series of economic and public policy challenges. Given the seniority-based pay system that prevails in many sectors of the Japanese economy, the aging of the labor force has direct implications for firm labor cost. The widespread use of lump-sum retirement allowances means firms face the prospect of large cash payments associ-

---

FIGURE 1–3 Birth and Death Rates in Japan

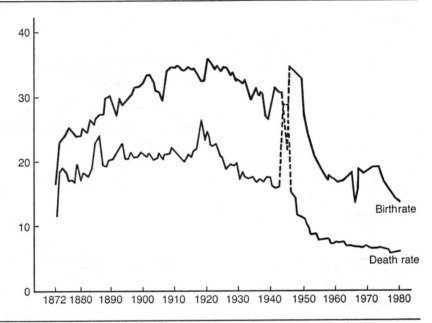

SOURCE: Policy Office for the Aged, Prime Minister's Secretariat, *Aging in Japan* (Tokyo: Japanese Government, 1983), p. 2.

---

ated with the increasing number of retirees. Firms have responded by attempting to reduce the generosity of these retirement plans and by shifting to a greater reliance on pensions, which offer annuitized benefits and, therefore, spread the expenditures for retirement benefits over a number of years. Pension benefit formulas have been lowered in an effort to reduce labor costs.

The changing demography also has implications for retirement age policies and the financing of the social security system. Indicative of the increasing cost of financing the social security program is the increasing number of persons age 65 and over relative to persons of working ages 20 to 64. This ratio has risen from 10 percent in 1950 to a projected 44.8 percent in 2020. As illustrated in Table 1–1, the aging of the Japanese population has been very rapid. While the United States and other developed countries had many years to respond to the aging of their populations, Japan must adapt to an aging population in a matter of only a few decades. The pace of aging may intensify the economic reactions to population aging.[6]

FIGURE 1–4   Trend in Life Expectancy at Birth in Japan

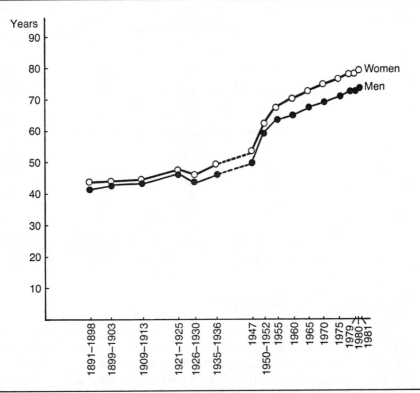

SOURCE: Policy Office for the Aged, Prime Minister's Secretariat, *Aging in Japan* (Tokyo: Japanese Government, 1983), p. 2.

The impact of population aging on public pension systems is reflected in the increased costs of real and relative pension expenditures throughout the developed world. However, the expected increase in Japan is much greater than it is in the other developed countries. Table 1–2 shows that the real pension expenditures in Japan are expected to increase from an index of 100 in 1980 to 1,314 in 2025. Increases in the United Kingdom, the United States, and France are expected to reach only 290 to 325. As a percentage of gross domestic product (GDP), pension expenditures are expected to more than triple in Japan while rising by less than 75 percent in these other developed countries. The primary factor driving these increases in expenditures is the aging of the population, which leads to a projected annual increase in pension expenditures of 5.9 percent in Japan.[7]

TABLE 1–2 Projection of Pension Expenditures: Developed Countries

Country	1980	2000	2010	2025
		Index of Real Pension Expenditures		
Canada	100	154	189	317
France	100	175	230	325
West Germany	100	180	218	300
Italy	100	198	285	498
Japan	100	430	787	1,314
United Kingdom	100	159	199	290
United States	100	145	178	306
		Index of Ratio of Pension Expenditure to GDP		
Canada	100	89	89	123
France	100	110	115	130
West Germany	100	129	140	154
Italy	100	121	138	171
Japan	100	229	307	319
United Kingdom	100	115	124	144
United States	100	92	90	110

SOURCE: Peter Heller, Richard Hemming, and Peter Kohnert, *Aging and Social Expenditures in the Major Industrial Countries, 1980–2025* (Washington, D.C.: International Monetary Fund, 1986), p. 31.

FRAMEWORK FOR ANALYSIS

The Japanese retirement system differs substantially from that developed in the United States. Although it was developed more recently, this retirement system is now being subjected to the stress of an aging population that will confront the United States only after 2010. This analysis will provide a detailed discussion of the public and private retirement programs in Japan and examine how they are responding to the aging of the population.

Throughout this analysis, differences between the Japanese system and that of the United States are highlighted. Each system is closely linked to prevailing industrial relations practices and government policies concerning the employment of older workers. This study indicates that two different retirement systems have arisen in these highly developed economies. Both countries have faced the rising costs of providing retirement income, and both have responded by modifying their social security systems. In direct contrast to the European countries, both the United States and Japan have raised pensionable ages and are attempting to maintain high rates of labor force participation by older persons. Successful programs in one country may provide guidance for policy reforms in the other. Thus, it is important for policymakers and researchers in the United States to be familiar with the Japanese experience.

ENDNOTES

1. See John Durand, *The Labor Force in Economic Development* (Princeton, N.J.: Princeton University Press, 1975); and Robert Clark and Richard Anker, "Labour Force Participation of Older Persons: An International Comparison," International Labour Office, World Employment Programme Research, Working Paper No. 171, December 1989.

2. For a detailed review of Japanese population aging and its causes, see Linda Martin, "The Graying of Japan," *Population Bulletin* 44, no. 2 (July 1989).

3. Prime Minister's Secretariat, *Aging in Japan* (Tokyo: Japanese Government, 1983). For an analysis of the causes of mortality declines in Japan, see Machiko Yanagishita and Jack Guralnik, "Changing Mortality Patterns that Led Life Expectancy in Japan to Surpass Sweden's: 1972–1982," *Demography*, November 1988, pp. 611–24.

4. Ishi Hiromitsu, "Why Tax Reform Now?" *Japan Echo*, Summer 1988. p. 37.

5. Unpublished data compiled by Professor Naohiro Ogawa, College of Economics, Nihon University, Tokyo. Data are from the Basic Survey of Wage Structure, various years.

6. The aging of the population is viewed as an important factor determining future government fiscal policy. In reviewing the current debate over tax reform, Professor Hiromitsu, "Why Tax Reform Now?" p. 38, concludes that "preparing for the graying of Japanese society is the most important goal of tax reform." For a general discussion of the economic effects of population aging, see Robert Clark and Joseph Spengler, *The Economics of Individual and Population Aging* (New York: Cambridge University Press, 1980).

7. Peter Heller, Richard Hemming, and Peter Kohnert, *Aging and Social Expenditures in the Major Industrial Countries, 1980–2025* (Washington, D.C.; International Monetary Fund, 1986), pp. 30–33.

CHAPTER 2

Work and Retirement

LABOR MARKETS AND EMPLOYMENT CONTRACTS

The Japanese labor market for regular, full-time male workers is characterized by long-term employment with a single employer, combined with a comprehensive compensation system.[1] This means many workers join a particular firm immediately after graduating from school and remain with that company until the mandatory retirement age. Turnover among Japanese workers is lower than it is in the United States, and, as a result, the average length of job tenure is longer.[2]

The employer trains the worker and provides a wide array of employee benefits. Bonuses are generally paid in addition to monthly earnings.[3] The annual bonus is typically equivalent to one third of annual earnings. In 1988, bonuses averaged 3.4 months of earnings.[4] Bonuses vary with the profitability of the company and are typically paid during the summer and at the end of the year.[5] The bonus system allows firms to reduce total compensation (earnings plus bonuses) during periods of reduced demand. This flexibility in total compensation facilitates the retention of workers during economic downturns. However, during the 1980s, bonuses had been a relatively constant multiple of monthly earnings. Thus, it would seem that bonuses have virtually become a fixed component of annual salaries.

Female workers tend to have less job tenure and lower salaries. The intermittent pattern of lifetime labor supply of women differs substantially from the long-term relationship between male workers and their employers. Part-time workers, whether male or female, have

TABLE 2-1 Proportion of Employees Who Are Part-Time Workers (by firm size)

Size of Firm	1975	1978	1979	1980	1984	1985
Total	2.9%	4.7%	6.0%	5.8%	7.6%	8.6%
5–29	5.4	7.0	9.8	7.9	10.0	11.4
30–99	3.2	5.4	7.3	6.7	11.2	11.2
100–299	2.9	5.1	6.0	6.8	6.9	8.9
300–999	1.6	3.5	4.8	6.3	6.0	7.3
1,000 or more	1.4	3.1	2.9	3.8	5.3	5.7

SOURCE: Ministry of Labor, Survey on Employment Trend, as reported in Japan Institute of Labor, *Japanese Working Life Profile* (Tokyo: Japanese Government, 1987), p. 72.

higher rates of turnover and are often excluded from many company benefits. In 1981, a special survey of the labor force found that 94 percent of male employees were regular workers, but only 74 percent of females were regular employees. Nonregular employees include part-time workers and other employees who are not regular employees. The proportion of workers who are part time is larger for small firms; however, the use of part-time workers has increased for all firm sizes.[6] Table 2–1 indicates that the proportion of all employees who are part time increased from 2.9 percent in 1975 to 8.6 percent in 1985.

For regular workers, cash earnings grow with seniority, and the level of pay is often tied more to years of service than to performance. Automatic salary increases are guaranteed in return for satisfactory service and remaining on the job. The seniority-based pay system in Japan has attracted considerable attention from analysts in the United States. The uniqueness of this compensation method is debatable, as most employers in the United States and other developed countries have, to some extent, seniority-based pay systems. In addition, recent surveys conducted by the Ministry of Labor indicate that an increasing proportion of firms are using ability or merit pay systems.

Most firms specify a definite end to the career by imposing a mandatory retirement age. Traditionally, this age of compulsory retirement has been relatively young. Until the 1970s, 55 was the most common age of mandatory retirement. In general, retirement benefits are paid to departing workers so that the career job is concluded with a final lump-sum payment. Most companies' retirement benefit plans use uniform percentages or formulas for all workers to determine lump-sum retirement allowances, bonuses, salary increases, and pension benefits.[7]

This system of industrial relations has been undergoing substantial change in response to the aging of the population and the increased number of retirees. Evidence indicates firms are responding to the aging of the population by actions that tend to reduce the compensation of older workers. These actions include reducing the wage increase after age 50 and revising downward formulas for retirement benefits. To further counteract the effect of rising costs of an older labor force, some firms have begun to offer early retirement incentives.[8]

The system of long-term employment is much more prevalent in large firms. Larger firms also pay higher total compensation, are more likely to have mandatory retirement policies, and are more likely to offer retirement payments. Larger companies in the United States also pay higher total compensation and are more likely to offer retirement benefits.

The earnings differential among companies of various sizes in Japan has been widening since 1965. In 1985, scheduled earnings in firms with 1,000 or more workers was 15 percent higher than in companies with 100 to 999 employees and 21 percent higher than in firms with 10 to 99 employees. The differential is a function of age, as young workers in small firms have almost the same earnings as those in large firms. The differential widens with age until the late 50s and then begins to decline.[9]

The value of nonstatutory employee benefits including pensions and retirement allowances is much greater for large companies. As a result, large firms have lower turnover rates and tend to invest more in training their workers. For example, the average tenure for a male manufacturing worker aged 40 to 44 in 1986 was 21.3 years for workers in firms with 1,000 or more workers, compared to 17.6 years in firms with 100 to 999 employees and only 12.7 years in firms with 10 to 99 employees.[10] Thus, throughout this analysis, distinctions will be drawn based on the size of the employer.

MANDATORY RETIREMENT

The Japanese industrial relations system is characterized by job security and annual pay increases for regular workers up to the age of mandatory retirement. Virtually all firms with more than 30 employees require workers to retire at some specified age. Despite these policies, labor force participation rates of older persons in Japan is the highest in the developed world. This section examines the use of mandatory retirement as a personnel policy among Japanese firms. The analysis considers how the age of mandatory retirement has changed over time with the aging of the population and in response to government policies encouraging delayed retirement.

In Japan, it is very difficult for employers to discharge or lay off regular employees except when the worker has engaged in some form of misconduct. The guarantee of continued employment coupled with a seniority-based compensation system encourages firms to establish a formal end to the employment arrangement at some specified age. Worker salaries are increased each year regardless of performance. Such seniority pay systems may result in older workers being paid more than the value of their productivity, thus providing firms with an incentive to force workers to retire. If older workers were permitted to remain on the job indefinitely, labor costs would continue to rise more rapidly than productivity. With this compensation system, firms have a strong financial incentive to set a definite date for the end of the employment contract. The link between final pay and retirement benefits also provides an incentive for firms to encourage or force older workers to leave the firm.

The compulsory retirement system was first instituted at the end of the 19th century. The mandatory retirement age was typically set at 55. During this period, life expectancy was much lower and turnover was greater. In this setting, mandatory retirement coupled with a lump-sum retirement benefit was used as a reward for remaining on the job. Since 1945, the mandatory retirement system has become an important firm personnel policy enabling firms to remove older workers from their payrolls and, in the process, reduce labor costs and increase promotional prospects for younger workers.[11]

Mandatory retirement is widely used in all sectors of the Japanese economy. In 1988, 88 percent of all firms with 30 or more employees required workers to retire at some specified age. The proportion of firms with such policies has increased steadily since 1973, when only two thirds of firms had adopted policies of compulsory retirement for their workers. Mandatory retirement is more prevalent among large firms, with virtually all firms (over 99 percent) with 300 or more employees adopting such a policy. Even for smaller firms, coverage rates are quite high—97 percent of firms with 100 to 299 employees and 84 percent of firms with 30 to 99 employees have specified mandatory retirement ages.

Government Policy toward Mandatory Retirement

As noted above, the traditional mandatory retirement age has been 55. As late as 1967, 63 percent of all firms imposed an age 55 retirement policy, with most other firms adopting a compulsory retirement age between 56 and 60. Over time, the retirement age has been raised partially in response to government policies encouraging delayed retirement. The first such legislation encouraging the continued employment of older workers was passed in 1973. This law provided encouragement for firms to voluntarily extend their age limits. In April 1986, the Stabilization of Employment for Elderly Persons Act was passed by the Diet, the National Assembly of Japan. This legislation states that firms are to initiate policies to raise the mandatory retirement age to 60. This act promoted as policy the establishment of a minimum age for mandatory retirement at age 60 and encouraged the raising of this minimum from 60 to 65.[12] However, no penalties are imposed on firms that do not raise their retirement age to meet this objective. Thus, many companies continue to impose mandatory retirement prior to age 60.

The prevalence of mandatory retirement as a personnel policy in Japan differs substantially from current U.S. practices. Prior to the 1980s, mandatory retirement policies were widely used in conjunction with employer pensions by many firms in the United States.[13] The Age Discrimination in Employment Act, passed in 1967, precluded the use of mandatory retirement prior to age 65 in most jobs. In 1978, this act was amended, raising the earliest age of legal mandatory retirement to 70. Further amendments to the Age Discrimination in Employment Act were passed in 1986. These amendments outlawed the use of mandatory retirement altogether as a personnel policy at any age for most jobs.

In both countries, the government has tried to encourage greater work opportunities for older persons by raising permissible ages for mandatory retirement. In the United States, the elimination of mandatory retirement has had very little effect on the work rates of older persons. This limited effect is due to the high incidence of early retirement.[14] In Japan, persons are much more likely to work up to the age of mandatory retirement. Therefore, raising this age will tend to have a greater impact on the probability that older workers will remain with the firm.

Distribution of Mandatory Retirement Ages

By 1987, the modal retirement age in Japan had risen to 60, with 54 percent of firms adopting this age and only 23 percent still using 55 as the mandatory age of retirement.[15] Changes in the distribution of mandatory retirement ages between 1972 and 1987 are shown in Table 2–2. Large firms tend to have later retirement ages than smaller firms: 86 percent of firms with 5,000 or more employees now adopt age 60 as the compulsory retirement age, while only about three fifths of firms with less than 1,000 employees set age 60 as the mandatory

TABLE 2–2 Distribution of Mandatory Retirement Ages (percent of companies)

	Age					
Year	54 or Lower	55	56–59	60	61–64	65
1972	0.7%	57.9%	18.3%	21.7%	0.3%	1.1%
1978	0.1	41.3	19.4	33.7	0.4	4.4
1982	0.5	35.5	18.2	43.0	0.8	2.0
1986	0.1	26.7	16.6	52.5	2.3	1.8
1987	0.3	23.0	18.0	53.9	2.3	2.5

SOURCE: *Survey of Employment Management,* various years.

TABLE 2–3 Mandatory Retirement Age and Size of Firm: 1989*

	Age						
Firm Size	54 or Lower	55	56–59	60	61–64	65	66 or older
All firms	0.5%	20.7%	17.0%	57.6%	1.1%	2.9%	0.3%
30–39	0.7	21.8	16.3	56.4	1.1	3.4	0.3
100–299	0.2	20.0	18.5	57.9	1.0	2.2	0.2
300–999		15.6	19.0	62.8	1.8	0.8	
1,000–4,999		10.4	14.5	74.0	0.7	0.4	
5,000 and over		4.9	8.7	86.4			

*Entries represent the percentage of firms with a mandatory retirement policy that have adopted the specified age.

SOURCE: Kiyoshi Murakami, "Severance and Retirement Benefits in Japan," in *Pension Policy: An International Perspective,* John Turner and Lorna Dailey (Eds.) Washington, D.C.: U.S. Government Printing Office, forthcoming.

retirement age (see Table 2–3). Smaller firms are much more likely to continue to use 55 as the mandatory retirement age. Almost one fifth of firms with less than 1,000 workers set 55 as the age of compulsory retirement, and another 15 to 19 percent of these firms use ages 56 to 59.

The variation in average retirement ages by industries is shown in Table 2–4. The average retirement age is the average for firms in each industry unweighted for size of the firm. The data illustrate that the mandatory retirement age has risen in each industry. In 1986, the lowest industry average retirement age was 57.7 (mining), and the highest average age of compulsory retirement was 58.9 (services). For all firms, the average retirement age rose from 56.5 in 1967 to 58.6 in 1987.

WORK AFTER RETIREMENT

Despite the almost universal use of mandatory retirement require ments at age 60 or younger, the labor force participation rates of older

TABLE 2–4 Average Retirement Age by Industry*

Industry	1972	1978	1982	1986
Mining	56.1	56.0	56.4	57.7
Construction	57.3	58.4	58.5	58.7
Manufacturing	56.6	57.2	57.8	58.4
Trade	56.4	57.3	57.2	58.0
Finance and insurance	56.6	56.6	56.8	58.1
Real estate	57.0	57.2	58.3	58.7
Utilities	55.3	57.2	57.4	58.8
Transportation, communication	56.0	56.6	57.7	58.4
Services +	—	57.8	58.5	58.9

*Average retirement age for each industry is calculated by finding the age based on the portion of firms in each industry using various ages. This technique does not weight for the number of persons covered by each retirement age.

+ The service sector was not included in the 1972 survey.

SOURCE: *Survey on Employment Management,* various years, and my calculations.

TABLE 2–5 Labor Force Participation Rates of Men Aged 65 and Older

Country	1950	1960	1970	1980	1985*
Australia	32.7%	28.2%	21.8%	13.5%	12.7%
Belgium	19.4	9.4	6.2	4.6	4.4
Canada	40.9	30.4	21.7	14.6	13.8
Denmark	38.0	32.4	26.9	15.3	14.2
France	37.2	26.1	15.0	6.0	5.6
Germany	27.5	21.4	16.7	4.9	4.7
Italy	46.6	27.5	14.5	7.5	6.8
Japan	54.5	54.5	54.5	45.8	42.7
Netherlands	31.5	20.4	11.4	4.5	4.2
Sweden	36.4	27.7	19.0	10.3	9.7
United Kingdom	34.4	26.6	18.8	11.0	10.6
United States	45.0	33.9	25.5	19.1	18.2

*Labor force participation rates for 1985 are based on projections by the International Labor Office. Actual rates for 1985 tend to deviate somewhat from these projections.

SOURCE: United Nations, *World Demographic Estimates and Projections, 1950–2025* (New York: United Nations, 1988).

Japanese are among the highest in the developed world. Table 2–5 shows that the participation for Japanese men age 65 and older was 42.7 percent in 1985, which is more than 30 percentage points higher than that for most of the European countries and 25 percentage points higher than for older men in the United States. Although their participation rates have fallen during the last four decades, this disparity in the work rates of older men in Japan relative to other developed countries has widened considerably since 1950.[16]

How can we reconcile the widespread use of mandatory retirement and the high labor force participation rates of older Japanese? The explanation of this apparent paradox lies in the distinction between retiring from a career job and leaving the labor force altogether. Many companies have instituted reemployment policies where workers who have passed the age of mandatory retirement are rehired. In 1986, 70 percent of companies with 30 or more employees reported having some type of employment extension or reemployment program. Such personnel policies are more prevalent among smaller firms.[17] These returning workers are typically employed in lower-ranking jobs and at a lower salary. In addition, they do not receive the automatic pay increases associated with further seniority. Thus, some workers are mandatorily retired but remain employed by the same firm.

The practices of reemployment or employment extension make older workers more desirable to firms and, therefore, increase the demand for them. These policies give employers increased flexibility in determining personnel decisions, lower labor costs, and enhance promotional prospects for younger workers. There is some evidence that firms are beginning to downgrade older workers even prior to the age of mandatory retirement. This seems to be occurring in firms that are raising their age of compulsory retirement.[18]

Extending employment past the age of mandatory retirement clearly increases job opportunities for older workers. However, these workers receive wage reductions, lower benefits, and job reassignment. Such practices would clearly be illegal in the United States under the Age Discrimination in Employment Act. This act protects workers over age 40 from adverse personnel policies based solely on their age. Thus, firms in the United States cannot arbitrarily reduce wages of older workers or demote them at a specific age. The inability to adjust wages and job responsibilities may reduce the demand for older workers in the United States.

Another common personnel policy in Japan is for older workers to leave their current employer, who then helps them find a new job with one of its subsidiary firms. Still other "retiring" workers start their own business or find jobs with new employers. The labor force data clearly reveal that older workers who are mandatorily retired in their 50s do not stop all work and leave the labor force. Instead, most of these "retirees" find new jobs and remain at work for many more years.

GOVERNMENT EMPLOYMENT POLICIES

The Japanese government has attempted to entice firms to raise the age of mandatory retirement to 60 or even 65; however, legislation outlawing compulsory retirement prior to age 60 was recently defeated in the Diet. In addition, the government has encouraged the hiring and retention of older workers through subsidies to firms. A series of government actions beginning in 1966 have been aimed at increasing employment opportunities for older persons. The Employment Promotion Measures Act of 1966 set guidelines for hiring workers age 35 and over. Firms were encouraged to comply and were offered subsidies, but they could not be forced to meet government employment targets. Employment goals for older workers were revised and extended in 1971.

Subsidy schemes include wage subsidies to firms hiring older workers through public placement agencies, subsidies for retaining employees past age 60, payments to firms that maintain a specified ratio of workers age 60 to 65 to total employees, and lump-sum payments to firms hiring persons age 60 to 65 within three months of their retirement. Recently, the government has instituted a system of subsidies to new firms that use large numbers of retirees. Employment subsidies may be a one-time payment to firms hiring or retraining older workers or a continuing monthly payment.[19]

A continuing objective of public policy is to promote a higher mandatory retirement age to enable persons to remain with their career firm until age 65. To facilitate work until older ages, the government is attempting to expand employment options available to older workers and to provide vocational retraining programs. The government also hopes to promote the redistribution of employment opportunities toward older workers and, hence, produce more leisure time for younger workers.[20]

Retired workers' job searches are aided by a series of Talent Banks that help older persons find new jobs. The first Talent Bank was established in Tokyo in 1967. Currently, there are 25 of these institutions nationwide whose objective is to help persons over age 40 with experience in management or specialized fields find reemployment with small- and medium-size firms.

These efforts are supplemented by 300 silver talent or manpower centers that attempt to place older persons in short-term or part-time jobs.[21] The first silver manpower center was established in Tokyo in 1975 with funds from local governments. Similar systems were introduced throughout Japan, and in 1980, the Ministry of Labor began to provide a subsidy to these centers. The silver manpower centers do not provide direct employment opportunities with firms in the community. Instead, the center enters into a contract with the employer to provide specific services, and then employment opportunities are allocated to center participants. Jobs tend to be temporary and service

TABLE 2–6 Age-Specific Labor Force Participation Rates

| | Males | | | | Females | | | |
| | Japan | | United States | | Japan | | United States | |
Age	1970	1985	1970	1986	1970	1985	1970	1986
55	96.1%	95.6%	91.8%	84.1%	57.2%	53.9%	52.6%	56.3%
56	95.4	94.5	90.7	80.9	55.8	51.7	48.2	54.5
57	94.8	93.5	89.1	79.7	54.4	49.9	50.0	51.3
58	93.0	91.9	87.7	77.2	51.7	47.9	47.6	48.4
59	91.6	89.5	87.5	73.4	49.7	45.7	45.9	46.1
60	89.4	84.4	83.9	69.2	47.2	42.5	44.0	42.3
61	87.9	80.0	81.2	66.2	45.4	39.8	38.5	37.8
62	86.1	77.6	73.9	53.5	43.3	37.8	36.1	31.8
63	83.7	74.8	69.4	44.3	40.8	35.3	31.9	28.1
64	80.7	71.7	64.4	39.4	37.9	33.0	28.4	25.2
65	78.1	67.5	49.9	30.8	35.9	30.5	22.1	18.6
66	75.2	63.8	44.7	27.6	33.2	28.1	19.3	15.4
67	72.1	60.5	39.4	24.0	30.9	26.2	16.2	13.5
68	68.7	57.2	37.7	20.7	28.5	23.9	15.0	12.4
69	65.0	53.5	34.0	20.7	25.6	21.7	12.9	10.5
70	60.7	49.7	30.2	17.1	23.7	19.3	12.2	8.4
71	55.6	46.1	27.9	15.3	20.1	17.3	9.8	7.1
72	51.3	42.7	24.8	14.1	18.1	15.5	8.6	6.9
73	47.5	38.5	22.0	14.5	16.2	13.3	7.7	6.1
74	42.9	35.1	19.1	12.7	14.3	11.8	6.4	5.8

SOURCE: The U.S. data are based on unpublished data from the Bureau of Labor Statistics. Japanese data are based on the Census of Population for 1970 and 1985.

oriented. The most common type of work is weeding public parks or private gardens. Members are paid by the center, are not employed by the contracting firms, are not covered by unemployment or accident insurance programs, and are not employed by any firm. Given these terms of employment, it is not surprising that these centers typically have more work opportunities than potential participants.[22]

LABOR FORCE PARTICIPATION RATES

Evidence suggests that the Japanese have a stronger attachment to the labor force than do comparable workers in other developed countries. Table 2–6 presents age-specific labor force participation rates by sex for Japan and the United States. Both countries show declines in participation rates for men between 1970 and the mid-1980s; however, the decline in the U.S. rates is greater than that experienced in Japan.

For the Japanese, the decline with an additional year of age in the proportion of men and women who are in the labor force averages around three percentage points per year between ages 55 and 74; however, the magnitude of this decline increases with advancing age. Inspection of the data does not reveal any large declines associated with mandatory retirement from a career job (ages 55 to 60) or with becoming eligible for Employees' Pension Insurance benefits (age 60) and National Pension benefits (age 65). By contrast, the U.S. data indicate sharp declines in participation at ages 62 and 65, which are key ages for receipt of social security benefits.[23] These data confirm the greater attachment to the labor force of Japanese workers at older ages and clearly indicate that mandatory retirement for a career job does not result in withdrawal from the labor force.

The actual work rates of the elderly conform to their expressed preferences for continued work. The extent of the desire for continued work by older persons is revealed in a survey by the Economic Planning Agency. This survey found that 78 percent of the respondents wanted to be employed at age 65, and 35 percent of the respondents wanted to continue to work until age 70.[24] Similar findings were reported from a 10-year longitudinal survey of older men in Tokyo. The men were first interviewed in 1975 when they were aged 50 to 54. When reinterviewed in 1985, 92 percent reported having left their career employer, but once retired, 87 percent immediately reentered the labor force. In 1985, 65 percent were still working, with 50 percent continuing at full-time jobs.[25]

The high rates of labor force participation occur despite the high average per capita income in Japan. In a recent study of participation rates in 151 countries, Clark and Anker estimated labor force participation rates of older men and women as a function of a series of socioeconomic variables. Their study showed that after controlling for these variables, the participation rates of elderly Japanese were substantially higher than those predicted by the regression model.[26]

Evidence suggests that workers who remain in the labor force suffer substantial reductions in earnings. A Status Survey of Employment and Life of Workers Reaching Retirement Age conducted by the Ministry of Labor in 1983 found that 30 percent of persons continuing to work after mandatory retirement had earnings reductions of 20 to 39 percent. Another 20 percent of these workers suffered earnings declines of 40 percent or more. The decline in earnings is greatest for persons who were previously employed by large firms.[27] These declines reflect the lower wages of workers who are reemployed by their former employer as well as the lower wages that older persons receive from new employers.

Despite high real income compared to other countries and wage cuts at mandatory retirement from career jobs, older Japanese continue to work. The high proportion of older persons who remain in the labor force does not appear to be due to low pension income (see Chapters 3 to 5).[28] Thus, the key economic factors do not explain the relatively high (by international standards) participation rates by older Japanese. The high work rates appear to be due to cultural and other socioeconomic differences influencing the work and retirement decisions. The current high labor force participation rates may reflect the lifetime experiences of current older Japanese. Persons currently age 65 and older lived through World War II and the postwar reconstruction. Future cohorts, having lived through the more prosperous era, should be more inclined to demand more leisure and retire earlier.[29]

RETIREMENT POLICIES IN AN AGING SOCIETY

The rapid aging of the Japanese population has caused changes in both public and private retirement policies. The continuing population aging has resulted in large past and projected future increases in expenditures for social security. In response to these cost increases, the benefit formulas of both the Employees' Pension Insurance and National Pension have been reduced. Discusssions are currently under way to raise the age of eligibility for benefits in these programs to further reduce projected cost increases.

In addition to changes in the social security system, the Japanese government has responded to demographic changes by seeking to encourage later retirement, thereby increasing the ratio of workers to retirees. Policies have included subsidies to firms hiring older workers, job placement assistance for unemployed older workers, and encouragement to firms to raise mandatory retirement ages. These efforts support the revealed preference for older Japanese to remain in the labor force. Thus, the response of the government to population aging has been to encourage delayed retirement to reduce the pressure on government spending for old age assistance programs.

The aging of the labor force and increased retirement ages confront Japanese firms with the prospect of rising labor costs. The seniority-based wage system means older workers tend to be more highly paid than younger workers, and this discrepancy increases as the age of retirement is raised. In many firms, retirement benefits are linked to final pay and are a function of years of service. In response to these rising labor costs, firms have begun to reduce the rate of wage increase for senior workers and to limit earnings used to determine retirement benefits. Pension systems are being altered, and firms are beginning to offer early retirement incentives. The industrial relations system is responding to both the aging of the population and changes in government policy.

This chapter has examined public and private retirement policies and how they have changed during the past 20 years. The aging of the population has produced an economic quandary for the government and for employers. The government is strongly encouraging continued work and the raising of retirement ages. Faced with higher labor costs resulting from an older work force, firms have attempted to revamp employee compensation to lessen the impact of an aging labor force. The following chapters focus directly on public and private retirement systems and how they have developed in conjunction with the aging of the Japanese society.

ENDNOTES

1. Detailed discussions of the industrial relations system in Japan are provided in Robert Cole, *Japanese Blue Collar: The Changing Tradition* (Berkeley: University of California Press, 1971); and Ronald Dore, *British Factory–Japanese Factory: Origins of National Diversity in Industrial Relations* (Berkeley: University of California Press, 1973). Haruo Shimada, "Perceptions and the Reality of Japanese Industrial Relations," *Keio Economic Studies* no. 2 (1982), pp. 1–21, presents an economic assessment of this traditional view of the Japanese system.

   A detailed description of employee compensation in Japan is presented by Yoshitaka Fujita, *Employee Benefits and Industrial Relations* (Tokyo: Japan Institute of Labor).

2. Masanori Hashimoto and John Raisian, "Employment, Tenure, and Earnings Profiles in Japan and the United States," *American Economic Review*, September 1985, pp. 721–35.

3. For an economic analysis of the bonus system, see Masanori Hashimoto, "Bonus Payments, On-The-Job Training, and Lifetime Employment in Japan," *Journal of Political Economy*, October 1979, pp. 1086–1104.

4. Data are from the Basic Survey of Wage Structure, 1988.

5. Japan Institute of Labor, *Wages and Hours of Work*, Japanese Industrial Relations Series no. 3, p. 16.

6. Japan Institute of Labor, *Japanese Working Life Profile* (Tokyo: Japanese Government, 1987), pp. 24, 73.

7. Fujita, *Employee Benefits and Industrial Relations*, p. 11.

8. For a comparison of the labor markets in the United States and Japan, see R. W. Bednarzik and C. R. Shields, "Comparing U.S. and Japanese Labor Markets," *Monthly Labor Review*, February 1989, pp. 31–42.

9. Japan Institute of Labor, *Japanese Working Life Profile*, pp. 28–29.

10. Ministry of Labor, *Yearbook of Labor Statistics: 1986*, pp. 110–11.

11. Haruo Shimada, *The Japanese Employment System* (Tokyo: Japan Institute of Labor, 1980), p. 16.

12. Kazuo Takada, "Evolving Employment Policies for Older Workers in Japan," in *When "Lifetime Employment" Ends* (Waltham, Mass.: Brandeis University, 1989), pp. 19–20, 26–28.

13. David Barker and Robert Clark, "Mandatory Retirement and Labor Force Participation of Respondents in the Retirement History Study," *Social Security Bulletin*, November 1980, pp. 20–29.

14. Richard Burkhauser and Joseph Quinn, "Is Mandatory Retirement Overrated?" *Journal of Human Resources*, Summer 1983, pp. 337–58.

15. A survey by the Japanese Federation of Employers Association of 410 companies in September 1988 found that 67.5 percent of firms had set mandatory retirement at age 60. *International Benefit Information Service*, March 1989, p. 29.

16. For a more detailed assessment of the participation of older persons around the world, see Robert Clark and Richard Anker, "Labor Force Participation Rates of Older Persons: An International Comparison," International Labour Office, World Employment Programme Research working paper, no. 171, December 1989.

17. Ministry of Labor, *Year Book of Labor Statistics: 1986*, p. 49.

18. Toshi Kii, "Retirement in Japan," in *Retirement in Industrial Societies*, ed. K. S. Markides and C. C. Cowper (New York: John Wiley & Sons, 1987), pp. 231–69. This downward mobility of older workers may start prior to the age of mandatory retirement. Masako Osako, "Downward Mobility as a Form of Phased Retirement in Japan," *Aging International*, December 1988, pp. 19–22, examines the process of reduced job status in Japanese companies. He reports that "preretire-

ment step down" is practiced in nearly half of the companies with 1,000 or more employees.

19. "Japan Expands Programs to Hire the Elderly," *Aging International*, December 1988, p. 7; also see Takada, "Evolving Employment Policies for Older Workers in Japan," for a detailed review of these subsidy programs.

20. Economic Planning Agency, *Economic Management within a Global Context* (Tokyo: 1988), pp. 45–46.

21. Kamata Satoshi, "Life after Retirement," *Japan Echo*, Special Issue 1988, pp. 28–33.

22. Shinya Hoshimo, "The Origins and Operations of Silver Manpower Centers," in When *"Lifetime Employment" Ends* (Waltham, Mass.: Brandeis University, 1989), pp. 41–88, provides a detailed review of silver manpower centers.

23. This point is also made in John McCallum, "Japanese Teinen Taishoku: How Cultural Values Affect Retirement," *Aging of Society*, March 1988, pp. 23–42. He reports declines in participation at the age of pension eligibility in Australia and the United Kingdom.

24. Satoshi, "Life after Retirement," p. 33.

25. "Occupational Mobility Following 'Retirement' in Japan," *Aging International*, December 1988, p. 7.

26. Clark and Anker, "Labor Force Participation Rates of Older Persons: An International Comparison."

27. Ken Sakuma, "Changes in Japanese-Style Labor-Management Relations," *Japanese Economic Studies*, Summer 1988, pp. 27–29.

28. John McCallum, "Japanese Teinen Taishoku."

29. A similar point can be made concerning the current high rate of savings among current older Japanese. Presently, the savings rates for persons over age 65 are only slightly below that for all households. Several researchers have speculated that future older households in Japan will be more like the elderly in other countries and have lower savings rates or actually begin to dissave. "The Silvering of Japan," *The Economist*, October 7, 1989, pp. 81–82.

CHAPTER 3

Social Security Retirement Benefit Systems

The Japanese social security system consists of the National Pension Plan, which provides a basic benefit to most persons, and five additional statutory pension programs that provide earnings-related benefits to retired employees in particular areas of the economy.[1] The Employees' Pension Insurance program, which covers most private employees, is the largest of these earnings-based benefit plans. Other earnings-related benefits are provided through statutory pension plans that cover specific groups of workers. These plans include the National Public Service Mutual Aid Association, Local Public Service Mutual Aid Association, Private School Teachers and Employees Mutual Aid Association, and Agricultural, Forestry, and Fishery Institutions Employees' Mutual Aid Association. These plans cover virtually all workers and their dependents.

The development of the Japanese social security system occurred much later than the implementation of such programs in Western Europe. For example, social security programs were instituted in Germany in 1889, in the United Kingdom in 1908, in France in 1910, in Sweden in 1913, and in Italy in 1919. By contrast, the first components of the Japanese system were instituted in the 1940s, only shortly after the start of similar programs in the United States in 1935.

The first continuing social security program to be established in Japan was the Employees' Pension Insurance system.[2] The Employees' Pension Insurance program was established in 1941 to cover private employees.[3] Other programs introduced in the 1950s and 1960s extended coverage to most employees. The largest of these programs is the National Pension Plan, which was implemented in 1961. Initially, the National Pension Plan covered only persons not included in other systems, primarily self-employed and family workers.

The social security system was fundamentally altered by the Pension Insurance Amendments enacted in April 1985. Principal objectives of the amendments were unification of pension systems, reduction of benefit costs, and establishment of pension rights for women. The changes mandated by this legislation became effective in April 1986. These amendments transformed the National Pension Plan from a pension plan for self-employed workers into a national retirement benefit system for all workers and dependents. The National Pension Plan now provides a flat benefit per year of contribution to all insured persons. The other pension programs cover different types of employees and provide earnings-related benefits to covered workers. Thus, under the new system, employees have both the basic benefit from the National Pension and an earnings-related benefit from their specific statutory plan. Self-employed workers and dependents are covered only by the National Pension.

The second objective of the 1986 legislation was to establish the social security systems on a sound financial basis for the long term and, thereby, reduce the projected rapid rise in the cost of the social security system.[4] The reforms altered the benefit formulas to gradually lower future benefits and, therefore, reduce the projected increases in the social security contribution rates.

The third objective was achieved by providing significant new coverage for women through their compulsory coverage in the National Pension Plan. Prior to the reforms, divorced women were often left without social security benefits. Under the new National Pension, all housewives are registered and will earn the right to be eligible to receive benefits in their own name. The increased reliance on the basic or flat benefit from the National Pension increased the importance of the wife's pension in the determination of family retirement income.

Table 3–1 presents a brief overview of the various social security programs. The Employees' Pension Insurance program and the National Pension Plan are by far the largest of these pension plans. In March 1988, the Employees' Pension Insurance program included 27.7 million insured workers, while the National Pension Plan covered an additional 30.6 million. These two pension programs covered 90 percent of the working population. Altogether, the mutual aid associations included 5.8 million insured workers with over 3 million in the Local Public Service Plan and just under 2 million in the National Public Service Plan. This chapter reviews the development of the social security system in Japan and examines the changes following

TABLE 3–1 Statutory Pension Schemes

	Private Sector	Wage or Salary Earners				Others
		Public Sector		Private Sector		
	Employees' Pension Insurance	National Public Service M.A.A.	Local Public Service M.A.A.	Private School Teachers and Employees M.A.A.	Agricultural, Forestry, and Fishery Institutions Employees' M.A.A.	National Pension
Name of scheme	Employees' Pension Insurance	National Public Service M.A.A.	Local Public Service M.A.A.	Private School Teachers and Employees M.A.A.	Agricultural, Forestry, and Fishery Institutions Employees' M.A.A.	National Pension
Year of enactment	1941–44	1958	1962	1953	1958	1959
Year of implementation	1944	1959	1962	1954	1959	1961
Persons insured	Employees in prescribed establishments	Employees of the central government, national railway, etc.	Employees of local government of various levels	Teachers and employees of privately established schools	Employees of cooperative and allied bodies in agriculture, fishery	All persons 20 to 60 except for students and pensioners
Administration	Social insurance agency	The federation of national public service M.A.A.	The federation of local public service M.A.A.	M.A.A.	M.A.A.	National government

Note: M.A.A. = Mutual Aid Association.

SOURCE: Japan Foundation for Research and Development of Pension Schemes, *National Systems of Old-Age, Disability, and Survivors' Benefits in Japan* (Tokyo: 1986), p. 6, and updated information.

TABLE 3–2 Employees' Pension Insurance Contribution Rates: Males*

Date of Establishment	Total Contribution Rate†
March 1942	6.4%
October 1944	11.0
September 1947	9.4
August 1948	3.0
May 1960	3.5
May 1965	5.5
November 1969	6.2
November 1971	6.4
November 1973	7.6
August 1976	9.1
October 1980	10.6
October 1985	12.4
January 1990	14.3

*Female contribution rates have typically been lower than male rates. In 1989, the female rate was 11.75 percent; however, this rate is now gradually being raised so that it will equal the contribution rate of men in 1994.

†Rate paid half by employer and half by employee.

SOURCE: Japanese Ministry of Health and Welfare, "Outline of Recent Japanese Policy on Pensions: The Background and Measures for Reform" (Tokyo: Japanese Government, 1985), p. 33 and updates based on unpublished governmental reports.

the 1985 amendments. Because of their importance, the discussion concentrates on the Employees' Pension Insurance program and the National Pension Plan.

INCREASING COSTS AND THE NEED FOR REFORM

As in all developed countries, the maturing of social security systems and the aging of populations have required substantial increases in the real and relative costs of retirement benefits. Initially, the Employees' Pension Insurance program was established on a full-funding basis with total contribution rates of 6.4 percent in March 1942. Rates were quickly increased to 11 percent in 1944. In 1948, the program was reorganized and abandoned the full-funding principle. These changes, which shifted the Employees' Pension Insurance system away from full funding toward a pay-as-you-go method of financing, were implemented during a period of rapid inflation. These changes resulted in contribution rates being lowered to 3 percent. As shown in Table 3–2, rates have increased rapidly since that time, reflecting rising benefits and an aging population. Total contribution rates are divided equally between the worker and the firm.

The cost of the Employees' Pension Insurance system was rising rapidly in response to the maturing of the program and the aging of

TABLE 3–3 Trends and Projections of Participants, Beneficiaries, and Contribution Rates: Employees' Pension Insurance

Year	Number of Participants (in millions)	Number of Beneficiaries (in millions)	Beneficiaries / Participants	Contribution Rate before 1985 Law*	Contribution Rate after 1985 Reforms*
1960	13.2	0.04	0.3%	3.5%	
1965	18.4	0.2	1.1	5.5	
1970	22.3	0.5	2.3	6.2	
1975	23.6	1.0	4.4	7.6	
1980	25.2	2.0	8.0	10.6	
			Projected		
1986	26.9	3.4	12.7	12.4	12.4%
1990	27.9	4.6	16.5	12.4	12.4
2000	29.4	7.7	26.1	16.8	16.0
2010	28.5	10.8	38.0	24.9	23.4
2020	28.9	12.6	43.5	33.6	28.4
2030	28.2	12.8	45.4	38.8	28.9

*Contribution rates allow trust funds to decline to approximately one year's expenditures, in contrast to the seven years in trust fund in 1986. The trust fund stabilizes at around one year's expenditures.

SOURCE: Japanese Ministry of Health and Welfare, "Outline of Recent Japanese Policy on Pensions: The Background and Measures for Reform" (Tokyo: Japanese Government, 1985), pp. 34–36.

the population. Table 3–3 shows that the ratio of beneficiaries to active participants rose from 0.3 percent in 1960 to 8 percent in 1980. This ratio was projected to continue increasing to over 40 percent early in the next century. Without changes in the benefit formula, the contribution rate was projected to increase to 38.8 percent.

Expenditures and contribution rates for the National Pension Plan increased rapidly during this period. The trend in these rates prior to the 1985 reforms is shown in Table 3–4. Monthly contributions increased from between 100 and 150 yen in 1961 ($.28 and $.41 at an exchange rate of 360 yen per dollar) to 6,740 yen in 1985 ($28.26 at a rate of 238.5 yen per dollar).[5] During this period, the consumer price index rose by 350 percent. Accounting for inflation, the real 1985 contribution was 10 times the contribution in 1961.

Projections made by the Ministry of Health and Welfare indicated a rapid increase in the ratio of beneficiaries to active participants in the National Pension Plan. This ratio doubled between 1975 and 1980 and was expected to increase to 32.7 percent in 1990. The continued aging of the population was expected to increase the contribution in 1984 prices from 6,800 yen per month in 1986 to 19,500 yen in 2020 (see Table 3–5).

Despite the increase in contributions, reserves as a percentage of annual benefit expenditures in both of these programs declined rapidly. Reserves in the Employees' Pension Insurance system declined

TABLE 3-4 National Pension Contribution Amounts

Date of Establishment	Monthly Contribution Amount (yen)
April 1961	
Age 20–34	100
Age 35–59	150
January 1967	
Age 20–34	200
Age 35–59	250
January 1969	
Age 20–34	250
Age 35–59	300
July 1970	450
July 1972	550
January 1974	900
January 1975	1,100
April 1976	1,400
April 1977	2,200
April 1978	2,730
April 1979	3,300
April 1980	3,770
April 1981	4,500
April 1982	5,220
April 1983	5,830
April 1984	6,220
April 1985	6,740

SOURCE: Japanese Ministry of Health and Welfare, "Outline of Recent Japanese Policy on Pensions: The Background and Measures for Reform" (Tokyo: Japanese Government, 1985), p. 37.

TABLE 3-5 Trends and Projections of Participants, Beneficiaries, and Contribution Amounts: National Pension

Year	Number of Participants (in millions)	Number of Beneficiaries (in millions)	Beneficiaries Participants	Monthly Contribution Amount before 1985 Law* (yen)	Monthly Contribution Amount after 1985 Reforms* (yen)
1965	20.0	—		100	
1970	24.3	—		450	
1975	25.9	2.7	10.6%	1,100	
1980	27.6	5.3	19.3	3,770	
Projected					
1986	26.4	7.6	28.8	6,800	6,800 (1984 prices)
1990	26.2	8.6	32.7	10,400	8,000
2000	26.7	9.7	36.3	15,000	11,000
2010	24.5	10.3	42.1	18,500	13,000
2020	23.8	9.7	41.0	19,500	13,000
2030	23.3	9.2	40.0	19,500	13,000

*Contribution amounts are sufficient to maintain trust funds at one year's expenditure in long run.

SOURCE: Japanese Ministry of Health and Welfare, "Outline of Recent Japanese Policy on Pensions: The Background and Measures for Reform" (Tokyo: Japanese Government, 1985), pp. 38–40.

TABLE 3–6 Social Security Trust Fund Reserves

| | Employees' Pension Insurance | | National Pension | |
| | Reserves at Start of Year | Reserves | Reserves at Start of Year | Reserves |
Year	(trillion yen)	Benefits Paid	(trillion yen)	Benefits Paid
1960	0.3	27.3%		
1965	0.9	23.7	0.1	67.4%
1970	3.6	22.0	0.6	37.0
1975	10.1	10.6	1.7	3.7
1980	24.4	7.5	2.4	1.5
1983	36.6	7.3	3.1	1.4
1985	45.5	7.9	2.7	1.1

SOURCE: Japanese Ministry of Health and Welfare, "Outline of Recent Japanese Policy on Pensions: The Background and Measures for Reform" (Tokyo: Japanese Government, 1985), pp. 33–37. Data for 1985 are provided in Lillian Liu, "Social Security Reforms in Japan," *Social Security Bulletin*, August 1987, p. 30; and Social Insurance Agency, *Outline of Social Insurance in Japan*, 1986.

from over 20 times annual benefits in the 1960s to 7 times annual expenditures in the 1980s. A steeper decline occurred in the relative funds of the National Pension Plan, where reserves declined from 37 years of benefits in 1970 to just over 1 year in the 1980s (see Table 3–6). Reserves in the National Pension fund have declined in actual magnitude as well as relative to annual expenditures.[6]

Funds collected under these social security plans are deposited in the Trust Fund Bureau of the Ministry of Finance.[7] These deposited funds receive an interest rate set by the Ministry of Finance (6.05 percent in 1988). Invested funds are redeemable in seven years. These funds are used for investment in housing, environmental sanitation facilities, welfare facilities, and other projects believed to raise the nation's standard of living.[8]

Changes in the Japanese economy were one cause of the more rapid decline in National Pension system reserves. As late as 1960, 60 percent of the labor force was composed of self-employed, farmers, and other family workers. These workers were covered by the National Pension. By 1987, employees accounted for 75 percent of the work force, while self-employed and other workers were only 25 percent of the total.[9] This decline in self-employment reduced the coverage base of active participants in the National Pension. The decreased number of workers contributing into the system placed added financial pressure on the National Pension by exacerbating the increase in ratio of beneficiaries to workers covered by this pension system.

The impacts of the 1985 social security reforms are shown in Tables 3–3 and 3–5. Without the benefit changes, the contribution rate for the Employees' Pension Insurance system was projected to rise to 38.8 percent. With the changes, the contribution rates were projected to stabilize at 28.9 percent in 2030. The monthly contribution amount for the National Pension in 1984 prices was projected to increase to 19,500 yen under the prereform benefit structure. With the reforms, contribution amounts were projected to peak at 13,000 yen per month.

The sharp increase in projected costs without changes was the primary force leading to the 1985 amendments. Even with these changes, Employees' Pension Insurance contribution rates were projected to more than double in the next 30 years, while contributions to the National Pension were expected to increase by over 90 percent. These remaining large increases are the primary reason for the current attempts to raise the age of eligibility for Employees' Pension Insurance benefits to 65.

NATIONAL PENSION

The National Pension Plan was established by legislation in 1959 and implemented in 1961. Initially, this public retirement program covered only self-employed workers and persons not covered by any other statutory pension. Participation by spouses of these workers was voluntary. The 1985 amendments transformed the National Pension system into a universal pension system offering a flat benefit to all covered persons. Currently, it insures all persons between the ages of 20 and 60 except students and old-age pensioners, who are excluded from compulsory coverage. It is possible for students and persons age 60 to 65 to voluntarily participate in the program. Since the 1985 reforms, wage and salary earners have been insured by both the National Pension Plan and one of the earnings-related pension plans for employees. These changes in coverage imply that the financing of the National Pension will no longer be affected by such shifts in the industrial structure of the economy as the decline in self-employed and family workers.

Financing of National Pension

Revenues for the National Pension Plan are derived from self-employed worker contributions, employer contributions for employees, and government contributions. Persons insured by the National Pension are divided into three categories. The first group consists of insured persons covered only by the National Pension Plan, such as self-employed and nonemployed persons. For example, a self-employed man's wife is in this group whether or not she participates in the family business. The second category of insured persons includes employees covered by the National Pension and another of the statutory pension plans. The third class of insured persons consists of dependent spouses of insured workers in category two who do not work for pay.

In 1986, the contribution for persons in the first class was set at 6,800 yen per month, and this rate was scheduled to increase annually by 300 yen until it reached 8,000 yen per month in 1990. The 1985 reforms mandated an actuarial review to determine new contribution rates necessary to maintain the plan on a sound financial basis. Legislation passed in December 1989 raised the contribution rate to 8,400 yen per month. Future contributions are to increase each year by 400 yen per month plus an increase to maintain the real value of contributions. Current legislation authorizes an actuarial review at least every five years. Payment by self-employed workers is made monthly by the worker at a designated government office or banking institution.

All persons who are not employees or their spouses are considered to be in this first category. Thus, unemployed workers, their spouses, and spouses of self-employed workers are in this category and are required to make monthly contributions. These contributions provide credited service and lead to benefits for such persons. The universality of the social security system depends on compliance by such persons. Whether these persons actually contribute to this system on a regular basis is yet to be determined. Workers and spouses could opt out of the system by not making the required payments. A large number of persons covered by the National Pension appear to be opting not to contribute to this pension plan.

Contributions for salaried employees in class two are collected by their employer in conjunction with their other pension scheme, for example, Employees' Pension Insurance. The contributions for dependent spouses are covered by the contributions of their spouse in category two. Thus, the contribution rate for the earnings-related pensions (discussed below) cover their participation in both the National Pension Plan and their earnings-related plan. The Employees' Pension Insurance system is responsible for financing the basic benefit on behalf of these participants. Similar contributions are made for participants in other pension plans.

Class one participants who are disabled or receiving means-tested benefits under social assistance programs are exempt from paying contributions. Payments that have been skipped due to this exempt status may be paid retroactively up to a maximum of 10 years. Even if contributions are subsequently not paid, these contribution-exempt periods are used to determine the retirement benefit (see below).

The total cost of the basic benefit is calculated annually and allocated among the pension programs in proportion to the persons insured in them. In addition to these contributions, government subsidies are used to fund benefits through the National Pension. These subsidies equal one third of the contributions from insured persons in category one and one third of the contributions from workers covered by other pension plans as they relate to the basic benefit.

Benefit Determination

Benefits under the National Pension take the form of a flat amount per month of contributory status to all qualified persons. In determining the qualifying period, the following are taken into account: (1) periods during which contributions to the National Pension have been paid (contribution-paid periods) or periods during which the person was exempted from payment as indicated above (contribution-exempt periods); (2) periods insured under an Employees' Pension Insurance program; and (3) periods during which the person was a dependent spouse of a person insured by an Employees' Pension Insurance program. Periods noted in (2) and (3) are regarded as contribution-paid periods.

Prior to the 1985 amendments, the National Pension paid a flat benefit to all qualified persons of

$$\text{Monthly benefit (in yen)} = 1{,}680\,[A + (B/3)] \div 12$$

where A is months of contribution-paid status and B is months of contribution-exempt status. This benefit formula is still used for all persons born before April 2, 1926.

A person born after April 1, 1926, is entitled to a basic old-age pension on reaching the age of 65 and having completed 25 years of qualified coverage.[10] Qualifying periods include coverage by the National Pension, Employees' Pension Insurance, or any of the mutual aid associations. Benefits may be accepted at age 60; however, persons accepting benefits prior to age 65 have permanently reduced benefits. Benefits accepted at age 60 are 58 percent of age-65 benefits. Delayed acceptance of the pension after age 65 increases monthly benefits.

The penalties for early retirement along with the increases for delayed acceptance are shown in Table 3–7. The gain for deferred acceptance in Japan is considerably greater than that in the United

TABLE 3–7 Early Retirement Penalties and Delayed Retirement Credits for National Pension

Age of Acceptance	Percent of Benefit at Age 65
60	58%
61	65
62	72
63	80
64	89
65	100
66	112
67	126
68	143
69	164
70	188

States. The gains from delaying acceptance are also greater than the actuarially fair increase in benefits associated with a reduced life expectancy at the older ages, that is, the wealth value of National Pension benefits increases with delayed acceptance. Despite this economic incentive to delay acceptance, most Japanese accept benefits prior to age 65.

When the 1985 reforms are fully implemented, the basic monthly benefit in 1984 prices will be 1,250 yen times the number of insured years. This yields a maximum monthly benefit of 50,000 yen ($210.50 at an exchange rate of 237.5 yen per dollar) for a worker with 40 or more years of coverage. These values are in 1984 prices as specified in the 1985 amendments. They are increased to reflect increases in the consumer price index. For persons retiring after October 1989, the maximum benefit is 55,500 yen per month. With an exchange rate of approximately 140 yen per dollar, this produces a benefit of almost $400 per month for a person with 40 years of coverage. Thus, an older couple could receive a combined monthly benefit from the National Pension of approximately $800 per month.

At the time of the social security reforms, the National Pension had not fully matured, that is, retiring workers had not been covered by the pension plan for their complete work life. The average length of insured status for persons retiring in 1986 was only 32 years. Under the old benefit formula, they would have received a monthly benefit of 53,760 yen (1,680 yen x 32). With the new formula, their benefit would be only 40,000 yen (1,250 x 32). Thus, the changes in the benefit formula would have created a sharp reduction in benefits for persons retiring just after the new formula went into effect relative

TABLE 3–8 Insurable Period for National Pension

Date of Birth	Insurable Period (months)
1926	300
1927	312
1928	324
1929	336
1930	348
1931	360
1932	372
1933	384
1934	396
1935	408
1936	420
1937	432
1938	444
1939	456
1940	468
1941 and after	480

SOURCE: Japan Foundation for Research and Development of Pension Schemes, *National System of Old-Age, Disability, and Survivors' Benefits in Japan* (Tokyo: 1986), p. 32.

to persons retiring just before the reforms. To smooth this transition, the new formula was gradually phased in by varying the length of the insured period. The transition benefit formula is

$$\text{Monthly benefit (in yen)} = \frac{50,000\,[A + (B/3)]}{C}$$

where C is the insurable period expressed in number of months. The value of C for persons born in various years is shown in Table 3–8. For all persons born after 1940, C will equal 480 months or 40 years.

Since 1973, the benefit amount has been automatically adjusted to changes in the cost of living if there has been an increase of 5 percent or more in the national consumer price index. An increase of less than 5 percent per year is carried over until the cumulative rise in the consumer price index exceeds 5 percent. This indexation is comparable to that enacted in the United States in 1972 and effective in 1975.

EMPLOYEES' PENSION INSURANCE

The Employees' Pension Insurance program was established in 1941. The initial program was designed so that full pension benefits could only be received after 20 years.[11] The program initially covered only male, manual workers in private establishments having 10 or more employees. Coverage was extended in 1944 to include salaried employees, female workers, and persons employed in establishments with five or more workers.

Currently, workers in private industrial or commercial enterprises that regularly employ one or more workers are compulsorily covered by the Employees' Pension Insurance system.[12] Firms not covered by this pension program include those in agriculture, forestry and fishery, restaurants and hotels, professions such as lawyers and public accountants, and theatre and other entertainment industries. Workers employed outside these covered firms may be covered by the Employees' Pension Insurance if the employer obtains the consent of at least half of his employees and the approval of the prefectual governor. All persons regularly employed in a covered firm are included in the Employees' Pension Insurance system if they are under age 65. To be eligible for a retirement benefit, workers must have 25 years of insured coverage in the plan. Persons over the age of 65 can maintain insured status to achieve the minimum requirement of 25 years of coverage. Short-term workers are excluded from coverage.

Benefit Determination

In 1953, the first pension benefits from the Employees' Pension Insurance system became payable. These initial benefits included only earnings-related benefits. A flat benefit that was not a function of years of service was introduced in 1954. Beginning in 1964, this flat benefit was made a function of years of service. For persons age 60 or older prior to the implementation of the 1985 amendments, the Employees' Pension Insurance system provided a flat benefit of 2,400 yen per month for each year of contribution.[13]

In addition to the flat benefit, an earnings-related benefit was provided by the prereform Employees' Pension Insurance. The benefit formula was a career average formula with wage indexation. The benefit for a person reaching age 60 in 1986 was determined by multiplying the average monthly insured remuneration times .01 times the number of insured years. Insured remuneration is based on average regular earnings excluding bonuses and overtime pay. On August 1 of each year, an insured person's average remuneration is calculated on the basis of the remuneration paid during the preceding three months.

A formula is used to convert actual earnings into insured remuneration. Insured remuneration is used to determine contributions to

TABLE 3-9 Schedule of Monthly Insured Remuneration for Employees' Pension Insurance System (000s of yen)

Average Remuneration		Class	Insured Remuneration
Equal or More Than	Less Than		
455	—	31	470
425	455	30	440
395	425	29	410
370	395	28	380
350	370	27	360
330	350	26	340
310	330	25	320
290	310	24	300
270	290	23	280
250	270	22	260
230	250	21	240
210	230	20	220
195	210	19	200
185	195	18	190
175	185	17	180
165	175	16	170
155	165	15	160
146	155	14	150
138	146	13	142
130	138	12	134
122	130	11	126
114	122	10	118
107	114	9	110
101	107	8	104
95	101	7	98
89	95	6	92
83	89	5	86
78	83	4	80
74	78	3	76
70	74	2	72
—	70	1	68

SOURCE: Social Insurance Agency, *Outline of Social Insurance in Japan* (Tokyo: 1988), p. 68.

and benefits from the Employees' Pension Insurance system. The formula has both minimum and maximum levels of insured earnings (see Table 3–9).

The prereform Employees' Pension Insurance benefit formula was

$$\text{Monthly amount (in yen)} = [2,400 \times Y] + [.01 \times E \times Y]$$

where E is average insured monthly remuneration and Y is the number of insured years.

In 1985, this system was substantially revised and coordinated with the National Pension Plan. The primary cost-reducing measure

TABLE 3–10 Coefficients and Unit Amounts under the Transitional Provisions of the Employees' Pension Insurance Scheme

Date of Birth*	Coefficient† (× 1/1,000)	Unit Amount (yen)
	(1)	(2)
1926	10.00	2,400
1927	9.86	2,323
1928	9.72	2,249
1929	9.58	2,176
1930	9.44	2,106
1931	9.31	2,039
1932	9.17	1,974
1933	9.04	1,910
1934	8.91	1,849
1935	8.79	1,790
1936	8.66	1,733
1937	8.54	1,676
1938	8.41	1,623
1939	8.29	1,570
1940	8.18	1,520
1941	8.06	1,471
1942	7.94	1,424
1943	7.83	1,379
1944	7.72	1,334
1945	7.61	1,291
1946	7.50	1,250

*Date of birth in 12-month period beginning April 2 of each year indicated and ending April 1 of the following year.

†Coefficient is the generosity factor in the benefit formula: retirees born prior to 1926 receive .01 times average earnings per year of contributions, and retirees born after 1946 will receive .0075 times average earnings per year of service.

SOURCE: Japan Foundation for Research and Development of Pension Schemes, *National System of Old-Age, Disability, and Survivor's Benefits in Japan* (Tokyo: 1986), p. 34.

imposed by these changes was the reduction of the benefit formula for future retirees. The flat benefit from the Employees' Pension Insurance eventually will be replaced by the new, lower National Pension benefit. To avoid sharp declines in the total benefit of participants in the Employees' Pension Insurance program, the reduction in the flat benefit component is gradually phased in through a 20-year transition period. Thus, it will be 2006 before the fixed benefit associated with coverage by the Employees' Pension Insurance is equal to the basic National Pension benefit. The reduction in this unit amount is shown in column (2) of Table 3–10. These values are reported in 1984 prices and adjusted upward with increases in the consumer price index.

The earnings-related benefit was reduced by altering the benefit formula. This modification ultimately reduces benefits by 25 percent. The benefit for persons reaching age 60 in 1986 was determined by multiplying the average monthly insured remuneration times .01 times the number of insured years. The benefit factor will be gradually lowered to .0075 in 2006 [see column (1), Table 3–10].

In 2006, when the reforms have been fully implemented, the earnings-related Employees' Pension Insurance benefit formula will be

$$\text{Monthly amount (in yen)} = .0075 \times E \times Y.$$

The average monthly insured remuneration is determined by all the insured remuneration during all insured years. When the retirement benefit is computed, past earnings are reevaluated to reflect increases in average wages of workers covered by the Employees' Pension Insurance system. The factors used in this reassessment of remuneration are revised at the regular actuarial review of the Employees' Pension Insurance system. Reviews must be conducted at least every five years.

The changes in the pension systems altered the benefit formulas of both the National Pension and the Employees' Pension Insurance. Their objective was to reduce future costs by restricting the growth in future benefits. The formulas in both pension systems included a factor indicating the number of years of credited service. Benefit increases had produced a formula that yielded a relatively high replacement ratio for years of covered service since the program had been instituted. Thus, the average married workers retiring in 1986 had 32 years of service and received a benefit equal to 68 percent of average lifetime earnings. With no change in the benefit formula, the replacement ratio would have risen to over 80 percent. The changes in the benefit formula were an attempt to maintain the replacement ratio at approximately the same level despite the expected increase in average covered service to around 40 years.

The effect of the 1985 amendments is shown by examining the pre- and postreform benefits for a single worker who earned average wages in the nonagricultural sector throughout his career (average monthly earnings of 254,000 yen), contributed for 32 years into the Employees' Pension Insurance system, and retired in 1986. This worker's total benefit would have been 158,000 yen per month in 1984 prices ($666 at an exchange rate of 237.5 yen per dollar). If married, the retiree would receive an additional 15,000 yen per month for a total of 173,000 yen per month. These benefits yield replacement ratios of 62 percent for the single worker and 68 percent for the married worker. The calculation of the benefit for a married retiree is shown in Figure 3–1.

FIGURE 3-1 Change in Total Social Security Benefits due to 1985 Pension Reform: Average Married Retired Employee*

	Prereform Monthly Benefit	
Total benefit	(1) Earnings-related component (254,000 × .01 × 32 years)	81,300 yen
	(2) Fixed-rate component (2,400 x 32)	76,800 yen
	(3) Increment for wife	15,000 yen
	Total benefit:	173,000 yen
	Replacement ratio: 68 percent	
	Benefit When Changes Fully Implemented	
Total benefit	(1) Earnings-related benefit (254,000 × .0075 × 40 years)	76,200 yen
	(2) Basic benefit, worker	50,000 yen
	(3) Basic benefit, wife	50,000 yen
	Total benefit:	176,200 yen
	Replacement ratio: 69 percent	

*Benefits are in 1984 prices. The worker is assumed to have average earnings in both examples of 254,000 yen per month. In 1986, the average worker had 32 years of credited service. When the changes in benefit are fully implemented, the average worker is expected to have 40 years of credited service.

SOURCE: Ministry of Health and Welfare, *Health and Welfare in Japan* (Tokyo: Japanese Government), p. 21.

If the benefit formula had remained unchanged, replacement ratios would have risen over time due to the increased coverage period. The average number of insured years of coverage at retirement will eventually reach 40. Under the prereform benefit structure, the monthly benefits for workers with average earnings of 254,000 yen per month would have risen to 212,600 yen for a married worker and 197,600 yen for a single worker. These benefits represent replacement ratios of 83 percent for the married retiree and 78 percent for the single retiree.

After the changes in the benefit formula have been fully implemented, future married retirees with a full work life of participation will receive a total benefit of 176,200 yen per month in 1984 prices, or a replacement rate of 69 percent. Figure 3-1 shows that the earnings-related benefit is substantially reduced, as is the worker's own flat benefit. By contrast, there is a large increase in the basic benefit of the wife. This restructuring of benefit formulas yields a benefit of only 126,200 yen for the single worker, or a replacement rate of 50 percent. This example indicates that single persons face larger benefit reductions than do couples.

Supplemental benefits are paid to beneficiaries with a dependent spouse under age 65 or children under age 18. The incremental benefit is 15,000 yen for a spouse and each of the first two dependent children. Each additional child increases the benefit by 5,000 yen. All values of these benefits are reported in 1984 prices as specified in the 1985 amendments. These values are automatically indexed to the consumer price index.

It is important to remember that these replacement rates compare social security benefits to gross preretirement earnings. Murakami estimates that the current benefit structure yields a benefit equal to about 80 percent of net aftertax earnings. This assumes a tax rate of 15 percent (including government taxes and social security contributions). If no changes had been made in the social security, total benefits would have exceeded net earnings as gross replacement rates rose and increases in taxes reduced net pay. Even with the 1985 changes, net replacement rates are expected to approach 100 percent in the future. The rise in net replacement rate occurs due to the increase in taxes on earnings as the costs of social security rise. Holding the gross replacement rate constant while reducing net earnings raises the net replacement rate.[14]

Retirement Age and Earnings Test

Men are able to start their Employees' Pension Insurance benefit at age 60. The basic benefit from the National Pension is not paid until age 65. The Employees' Pension Insurance system pays workers retiring at age 60 a combined benefit equal to the earnings-related benefit plus the basic benefit until age 65. At that time, the National Pension system begins to pay the basic benefit. Thus, employees can retire at age 60 without having benefits reduced. To qualify for an earnings-related benefit, an insured worker must satisfy the eligibility conditions for the basic benefit from the National Pension.

Prior to the 1986 legislation, women were able to receive a benefit beginning at age 55. The new laws raise the pensionable age for women by one year every three calendar years until 2000. At that time, the pensionable age for women will be 60, the same age as for men. Consideration has been given to raising the age of benefit acceptance to 65 for both sexes by 2010. The government proposed an increase in the retirement age as part of the 1989 actuarial review and subsequent legislation. This provision of the bill was deleted prior to its passage.

If a person eligible to receive a benefit continues to work beyond age 60, the combined benefit may still be paid but at a reduced rate. The amount of the reduction depends on the level of earnings. The rate of reduction is 20 percent if the average remuneration is less than 95,000 yen; 50 percent if earnings are between 95,000 and 155,000 yen; and 80 percent if earnings are between 155,000 and 210,000 yen. For earnings in excess of 210,000 yen, the benefit is suspended.

This structure of benefit reductions in response to earnings results in discrete drops in the net gain from working. As a result of the earnings test, the value of working declines from compensation paid by the employer to compensation minus the loss in pension benefits. This lower net compensation provides incentives for older persons to alter their working behavior.[15] This earnings test formula differs from the earnings test in the United States, which is uniform. The U.S. earnings test reduces benefits one dollar for each three dollars of earnings above a specified amount.[16] Just as in the United States, the earnings test in Japan is less restrictive for workers age 65 and older. Persons age 70 and older are not subject to the earnings test in the United States.

Evidence from both countries indicates that the earnings tests influence the labor supply decisions of affected workers. In the United States, the decline in labor force participation of older men has resulted in fewer people continuing to work and, therefore, actually facing the earnings test. In Japan, the participation rates of men age 60 to 64 continue to be 70 to 80 percent. Thus, many workers will be affected by the earnings test. Several recent studies have found that Japanese men do respond to the earnings test by altering their work behavior.[17] However, the labor force participation data reported in Chapter 2 do not indicate declines in participation rates associated with the social security programs.

Financing of Employees' Pension Insurance

Prior to the 1985 amendments, the Employees' Pension Insurance system was financed by equal contributions from employers and employees plus a general revenue subsidy equal to 20 percent of costs. The revised Employees' Pension Insurance system no longer receives transfers from the general fund. In 1989, the Employees' Pension Insurance contribution rate for male workers was 12.4 percent of the insured remuneration, half of which was paid by the worker and half by the employer. The contribution rate was 11.75 percent for female workers; however, this is scheduled to rise gradually until the rate is equal to that for men in 1994. These rates are similar to the 1989 U.S. total contribution rate of 11.06 percent of covered earnings for the old-age and survivors' portion of social security.

In December 1989, the tax rate for the Employees' Pension Insurance program was raised to 14.3 percent for men effective in 1990. In 1991, the rate will increase to 14.5 percent. This rate will remain in effect until the next actuarial review of the system in 1993 or 1994.

Employee contributions are collected by the employer through deductions from earnings. The employer is responsible for the payment of the employee and employer contributions. These payments are made through an approved financial institution, such as a bank or postal office. Overdue contributions may be coercively collected by the government.

The Ministry of Health and Welfare estimated that contribution rates would have risen to 38.8 percent by 2030 without the benefit reductions imposed by the 1986 reforms. With the benefit reductions, projections in 1985 indicated that the Employees' Pension Insurance contribution rates would peak at 28.9 percent in 2030. Even this increase implies a substantial increase in social security taxes. The projected rise in labor costs associated with higher social security taxes remains a cause for concern and is the principal factor driving the discussion to further increase the age of eligibility for social security benefits.

SOCIAL SECURITY: PROBLEMS AND PROSPECTS

The 1985 amendments to the Japanese social security system transformed these separate pension schemes into an integrated plan providing a basic benefit to all workers coupled with an earnings-related supplement for employees. Future benefits were substantially lowered in an effort to reduce projected costs.

When the new system has reached maturity, the replacement ratio for an employee with a dependent spouse and average insured earnings of 254,000 yen per month in 1984 prices ($1,069 at an exchange rate of 237.5 yen per dollar) and 40 years of coverage will be 69 percent. This follows from an earnings-related benefit of 76,200 yen (254,000 x .0075 x 40) plus the worker's basic benefit of 50,000 yen and the basic benefit for the spouse of 50,000 yen. This yields a total benefit (based on 1984 prices) of 176,200 yen per month ($742 per month), or 69 percent of the 254,000.[18] This relatively high replacement rate is based on the lifetime average of regular earnings excluding bonuses. Thus, in comparison to actual annual earnings including bonuses, the replacement rate is probably closer to 50 percent.[19]

In the United States, a worker with average earnings would receive benefits at age 65 equal to 42 percent of average earnings. If married and the wife, who is also age 65 or older, receives a spouse benefit, the family replacement ratio rises to 63 percent.[20] Thus, the typical Japanese retired employee with a nonworking spouse receives a somewhat lower replacement rate from social security than does a retiree in the United States. These replacement rates for Japan refer only to persons covered by both the National Pension and the Employees' Pension Insurance system. Self-employed workers are covered by only the National Pension and, therefore, will receive only the basic benefit for the worker and his spouse. Obviously, the replacement rate of these retirees depends on their preretirement earnings.

In addition, persons who experience years of unemployment, who switch between self-employment and salaried work, and who enter and leave the labor force will have fewer than 40 years of credited service in the Employees' Pension Insurance system and will not receive the maximum benefit. By comparison, the benefit formula in the United States drops the lowest five years of earnings from the determination of average income, and years of service do not directly enter the benefit formula. Therefore, several years outside the work force do not have much effect on the retirement benefit.

A second key feature of the social security reform was the changed treatment of women. The new system provides dependent spouses a basic benefit in their own right. Previously, a dependent wife insured under the Employees' Pension Insurance system was not entitled to disability benefits or to any benefit in the case of divorce. She was protected merely by her marriage to an insured worker. Under the new system, spouses are individually and compulsorily covered by the National Pension Plan and will be entitled to their own benefit. The discussion in this chapter has shown the importance of the spouse's basic benefit to total social security income. Sex differences in contribution rates and retirement ages are gradually being phased out.

Without the 1985 amendments, Employees' Pension Insurance contribution rates were projected to increase to 38.8 percent. Even with the 1985 modifications, the Employees' Pension Insurance contribution rate was projected to increase to 28.9 percent in 2025.

In 1989, the mandated five-year actuarial review of the social security system was conducted. New cost projections showed future social security costs rising more rapidly than anticipated. The required tax rate to finance the Employees' Pension Insurance program was projected to be 31.5 percent in 2020 instead of the 28.4 percent shown in Table 3–3. This large increase of over 3 percentage points was due primarily to a more rapid than anticipated aging of the population.

Required contributions for the National Pension were also found to be higher than expected.

In response to these higher projected costs, the government proposed to raise contribution rates for the Employees' Pension Insurance system to 14.6 percent and for the National Pension to 8,400 yen per month. The bill was modified in the Diet to increase the Employees' Pension Insurance contributions to 14.3 percent in 1990 and to 14.5 percent in 1991.

To further lower projected expenditures, the government proposed increasing the age of eligibility for pension benefits to 65. Raising the age of eligibility for benefits to 65 for both men and women is estimated to lower the projected contribution rate to 26.1 percent in 2020. The proposed increase in the age of eligibility for benefits was deleted from the bill in the Diet. It is expected that a similar proposal will be introduced at the next required review of the social security system in 1993 or 1994.

In summary, the National Pension Plan provides almost universal retirement coverage for the Japanese. The Employees' Pension Insurance and the other occupational pension schemes provide additional pension coverage to employees in most sectors of the economy. The level of income replacement for workers covered by the Employees' Pension Insurance system approximates that found in the United States. Benefits are automatically adjusted for inflation increases. The social security system redistributes income toward lower-paid workers through the use of the basic benefit, which is not determined by past earnings, and the use of minimum and maximum insured earnings.

The social security system has recently been modified in the face of rising costs due to the aging of the population and the maturing of the system. The continued rapid aging of the Japanese population implies that the contribution rates needed to finance the benefits from the formula specified in the present system will more than double in the coming years.

Some nongovernmental economists argue that the government projections of future costs are too optimistic. The Nihon University Population Research Institute's macroeconomic model of Japan estimates that future tax rates for the Employees' Pension Insurance program may rise to 40 percent of payroll. These projections indicate that Japan continues to face the same challenges confronting other developed countries concerning the high cost of providing adequate retirement income to an aging population. How the government resolves these issues will directly affect the rate of economic growth and the economic well-being of older persons in Japan.[21]

ENDNOTES

1. This section is based in part on Social Insurance Agency, *Outline of Social Insurance in Japan* (Tokyo: Japanese Government, 1988) and Japan Foundation for Research and Development of Pension Schemes, *National System of Old-Age, Disability, and Survivors' Benefits in Japan* (Tokyo: 1986).

2. In 1940, the Seamen's Insurance System was the first social security system to be implemented in Japan. The old-age pension component of this program was eliminated in 1986. Participants are now covered by Employees' Pension Insurance system.

3. This program was initially called Workers' Pension Insurance; however, the name was changed in 1944 to Employees' Pension Insurance.

4. The financial problems that confronted the social security systems are described by Mitsuhiro Fukao and Masatoshi Inouchi, "Public Pensions and the Savings Rate," *Economic Eye*, June 1985, pp. 22–25; and Yukio Noguchi, "Problems of Public Pensions in Japan," *Hitotsubashi Journal of Economics*, June 1983, pp. 43–68.

5. All conversions of yen values to dollars prior to 1988 reported in this study are based on the average exchange rate for the appropriate year as reported in the 1988 *International Financial Statistics Yearbook*. These rates are annual average exchange rates for the year. Rates for 1988 and 1989 are from the monthly issues of *International Financial Statistics* and are typical of the average exchange rate for a specified quarter of the year.

6. Lillian Liu, "Social Security Reforms in Japan," *Social Security Bulletin*, August 1987, p. 30. Also see Randall Jones, "The Economic Implications of Japan's Aging Population," *Asian Survey*, September 1988, pp. 958–69, for a review of the growth in the cost of social security in Japan. Alicia Munnell and Nicole Ernsberger, "Public Pension Surpluses and National Saving: Foreign Experience," *New England Economic Review*, March 1989, pp. 16–38, review the build-up of social security trust funds in Japan. They report that the combined Employees' Pension Insurance and National Pension reserves exceeded 18 percent of gross domestic product in Japan.

7. Beginning in 1989, some of these reserves will be invested with private financial institutions. The objective of this trans-

fer is to increase returns to the trust funds. Hiroshi Murakami and Shunichiro Toda, "Public Pension Schemes," *Benefits and Compensation International*, April 1989, p. 3.

8. Munnell and Ernsberger, "Public Pension Surpluses and National Saving," p. 27, provide a detailed accounting of the uses of these pension accounts.

9. Japanese Ministry of Health and Welfare, "Outline of Recent Japanese Policy on Pensions: The Background and Measures for Reform," p. 7; and Hiroshi Murakami and Shunichiro Toda, "Retirement," *Benefits and Compensation International*, April 1989, p. 3.

10. For the pension of spouses, months of coverage by the insured person in the Employees' Pension Insurance or any of the mutual aid associations prior to the 1985 reforms are counted toward this minimum coverage requirement. In addition, time spent abroad prior to 1985 can also be used to qualify for the minimum coverage. However, these periods are not included in the calculation of benefits.

11. Yoshitaka Yujta, *Employee Benefits and Industrial Relations* (Tokyo: Japan Institute of Labor, p. 10).

12. If the establishment is owned by an individual as opposed to a judicial person, coverage is compulsory if the firm regularly hires five or more workers.

13. Laurence Kotlikoff, John Shoven, Toskiaki Tachibanaki, and Kunio Takeuchi, "A Comparison of the Japanese and U.S. Pension Systems," unpublished paper, 1984, provide a review of the early development of the Employees' Pension Insurance system.

14. Kiyoshi Murakami, "Aging and Pensions in Japan," paper presented to Employee Benefit Research Institute Policy Forum, "Aging in Japan: Lessons for the U.S.?" July 26, 1989, Washington, D.C.

15. The labor supply effect of the earnings test in Japan is examined by Tetsuji Yamada and Tadashi Yamada, "Social Security and Earlier Retirement in Japan: Cross-Sectional Evidence," National Bureau of Economic Research Working Paper no. 2442, November 1987.

16. For evidence of the effect of the earnings test on retirement in the United States, see Alan Blinder, Roger Gordon, and Donald Wise, "Reconsidering the Work Disincentives of Social Security," *National Tax Journal*, December 1980, pp. 431–42;

and Gary Burtless and Robert Moffitt, "The Joint Choice of Retirement Age and Postretirement Hours," *Journal of Labor Economics*, April 1985, pp. 209–36.

17. For example, see Atsushi Seike, "The Effect of Employees' Pension on the Labor Supply of the Japanese Elderly," paper presented at Population Association of America meetings, Baltimore, March 1989.

18. Ministry of Health and Welfare, *Health and Welfare in Japan* (Tokyo: Japanese Government, p. 21).

19. Kotlikoff et al., "A Comparison of the Japanese and U.S. Pension Systems," found that the prereform replacement rate was 57 percent for workers with average monthly earnings. They estimated that including bonuses would reduce the replacement rate to 44 percent. Replacement rates were much higher for lower-paid workers with high years of credited service.

20. If the wife has been working, this replacement ratio overstates the total family social security benefit compared to total family earnings prior to retirement.

21. This underestimation of the government projections arises because of an underestimation of the pace of population aging, not accounting for the expected decline in labor force participation of older persons, and the use of a relatively high rate of economic growth.

CHAPTER 4

Tax Policy, Private Retirement Plans, and Lump-Sum Payments

Prior to the 1940s, the retirement income system in Japan consisted primarily of lump-sum retirement allowances. These retirement plans were payments by employers to employees leaving the firm for any of a variety of reasons, provided the worker had met certain minimum standards. They are more appropriately defined as severance pay plans. The first old-age pension programs were introduced in 1875; however, coverage was limited to military personnel. For the most part, the private pension system in Japan has developed in the last 25 years.

This chapter explores the coverage of Japanese workers by some type of private retirement program and examines the lump-sum severance plans in detail. The challenge of adjusting these programs to an aging population is shown to be one of the factors stimulating the shift to annuity pensions. Tax policy directly affects the choice of a retirement program by altering the cost of savings for retirement. Therefore, the first section of this chapter examines the Japanese system of taxation. The analysis concentrates on the effect of personal and corporate income tax on pension plans and other forms of savings for retirement.

TAX POLICY AND RETIREMENT INCOME

Individual retirement savings plans, along with company-sponsored and statutory pension programs, are structured within the framework of national tax policies. In many countries, governments have encouraged the establishment of formal retirement plans through the use of preferential tax treatment for pension plans. This section briefly describes Japanese tax policy and how it relates to the development of pensions and other retirement savings plans.

Japan and the United States have the lowest overall tax burden as a percent of gross domestic product (GDP) among the major OECD (Organization for Economic Cooperation and Development) countries. In 1985, tax revenues were 28 percent of GDP in Japan, compared to 29 percent in the United States.[1] The lower tax burdens in the United States and Japan were primarily due to lower social security costs stemming from their relatively young populations compared to the other developed countries. As examined earlier, population aging in Japan and the United States will increase these costs over the next three decades.

In Japan, taxes are levied by the national government, prefecture or state governments, and municipal governments. At the national level, most revenues are raised through personal and corporate income taxes. In fiscal 1988, 37.6 percent of tax revenues are estimated to be derived from the personal income tax and 30 percent from the corporate income tax.[2] Most of the other revenues are derived from a series of sales and excise taxes. The prefecture and local governments depend mostly on income and property taxes along with sales and excise taxes. The following analysis focuses on personal and corporate income taxes because these taxes most directly influence retirement savings plans.[3]

Personal Income Taxation

For taxation purposes, personal income is divided into 10 categories: interest income; dividends; real estate income; business income; employment income; retirement income; timber income; capital gains; occasional income, which includes gifts and prizes; and miscellaneous income, which includes royalties and fees for lectures. Retirement income includes only lump-sum severance payments and lump-sum payments from pension plans. Annuity income from a pension is included under miscellaneous income.[4]

Individual taxpayers determine their tax liability by first calculating their adjusted gross income. This is done within each income category. The first step is to subtract from gross receipts the allowable expenses of earning the income. Some of the income categories have special deductions for various types of income.

For most persons, earnings from employment will be their primary source of income. Employment income includes salaries, wages, allowances, and bonuses. Expenses cannot be deducted in an item-

ized manner; however, a special deduction is allowed for employment income. This deduction equals 40 percent of the first 1.65
million yen in earnings plus 30 percent of earnings between 1.65 and
3.3 million yen plus 20 percent of earnings between 3.3 and 6 million
yen plus 10 percent of earnings between 6 and 10 million yen plus 5
percent of earnings over 10 million yen. There is a minimum employment income deduction of 570,000 yen.

In addition to these deductions, specific exemptions are allowed
for loss on assets, medical expenses, losses from fire, and some dona-
tions. Of particular interest to this study is the deductibility of social
insurance premiums paid by the taxpayer for himself, his spouse, or
other relatives living with him. Since 1962, firm contributions to tax-
qualified pension plans have not been counted as current income to
employees and, since 1966, firm contributions to employees' pension
funds have not been counted as current income to the taxpayer.

Also, premiums on life insurance policies or contributions to tax-
qualified pensions are deductible in accordance with the following
formula: for premiums less than 25,000 yen, the entire premium is
deductible; for premiums between 25,000 and 50,000 yen, the deduction equals one half of the premium plus 12,500; for premiums between 50,000 and 100,000 yen, the deduction is one fourth of the
premium plus 25,000; and for premiums in excess of 100,000 yen, the
deduction is 50,000. All employee contributions to employees' pension funds are tax deductible.

Capital gains and savings receive special tax treatment in Japan.
A variety of deductions and exemptions result in low effective tax
rates on capital gains earned by individual taxpayers. Until 1987, individuals were permitted to establish savings plans in which the
earnings were tax exempt. Four types of savings plans were available
to taxpayers. First, interest accruing from postal savings plans when
the principal did not exceed 3 million yen were tax exempt. Second,
interest or distributions of profits from deposits, bonds, open-end
bond investment trusts, or specific stock investment trusts if the principal did not exceed 3 million yen were tax exempt. These accounts
were referred to as the Small Saving Tax Exemption. Third, interest
on central government and local government bonds not exceeding 3
million yen in total face value was tax exempt. Fourth, the System for
Savings for the Formation of Employees' Assets allows for tax-exempt
interest income or distribution of profits received from accounts set
up by employers for workers to accumulate assets particularly for
housing and pensions. Employees must establish savings contracts
and have contributions withheld from their earnings. The earnings

from these funds are only tax exempt when the principal does not exceed 5 million yen.

If an individual made maximum use of these four savings plans, he could have held up to 14 million yen in nontaxable forms. These maximums apply to individuals, so a family of four could have four times this amount in nontaxable investments.[5] Nagono estimated that over 70 percent of all personal savings in Japan were in one of these tax-exempt savings plans.[6] For most taxpayers, this tax-exempt savings system was abolished in 1987 and replaced with a flat tax of 20 percent of all interest income. All of the tax-exempt savings plans are still available to persons age 65 and older, fatherless families, and physically handicapped persons. The System for Savings for the Formation of Employees' Assets remains as a form of tax-exempt savings for employees.

Lump-sum retirement allowances are an important, one-time source of income to newly retired persons. Prior to 1989, retirees with 20 years or less of service with their employer could deduct from retirement income 250,000 yen per year of service. The minimum deduction from retirement income was 500,000 yen. If the length of service was more than 20 years, the deduction was 5 million yen plus 500,000 per year of service in excess of 20 years. Thus, a person with 30 years of service could receive a lump-sum severance payment of up to 10 million yen without incurring any tax liability.

These exemptions from retirement income have recently been raised. Currently, the exemption is 400,000 yen per year of service for the first 20 years plus 700,000 per year of service for job tenure in excess of 20 years. Thus, a retiree with 30 years of service could receive a lump-sum payment of 15 million yen tax free. In early 1989, this represented $116,000 at an exchange rate of 129.6 yen per dollar. For payments exceeding these values, 50 percent of the lump-sum payment in excess of the exempt amount is tax free, while the balance of the retirement benefit is taxed at regular income tax rates. Any benefits attributable to past employee contributions are not taxed.

Pension annuities from both social security and company pension plans are part of miscellaneous income and also subject to a special income tax deduction. In 1988, the deduction was composed of a flat amount plus a deduction that varies with the size of the annuity. To calculate the total deduction, first subtract 800,000 yen as a flat deduction. If the amount of the pension annuities after the flat deduction has been subtracted does not exceed 3.6 million yen, there is an additional, fixed-rate deduction equal to 25 percent of that amount. If the amount of the annuities after the fixed deduction exceeds 3.6 million yen but not 7.2 million yen, the fixed-rate deduction is 360,000 yen plus 15 percent of that amount. Finally, if the amount of the annuities after the flat deduction exceeds 7.2 million yen, the fixed-rate deduction is 1.08 million yen plus 5 percent of that amount. The minimum total deduction is 1.2 million yen for a taxpayer age 65 and older or 600,000 for a taxpayer under age 65. Benefits from tax-qualified pension plans attributable to employee contributions are not included in taxable income; however, all benefits from employees' pension funds are part of taxable income.

After these and similar adjustments have been made to each source of income, all of the types of income except retirement and timber incomes are added together. At this point, personal exemptions and deductions for specified expenditures are made. A taxpayer may subtract 330,000 yen as a basic deduction from his income for himself, his spouse, and dependents. In addition, a special exemption of 500,000 yen is allowed for persons age 65 and older; however, if annual income of an aged person exceeds 10 million yen, he is not entitled to this exemption.

After determining taxable income, the tax liability is calculated by using a progressive tax schedule. Marginal tax rates in 1988 ranged from 10.5 percent for income of less than 1.5 million yen to 60 percent on income in excess of 50 million yen. Prefectural and local income tax rates are then added to these rates. The maximum prefectural rate is 4 percent, and the maximum municipal rate is 14 percent. By statute, the total maximum income tax rate that anyone can be required to pay for these combined income taxes is 78 percent.

Tax legislation enacted in 1987 reduced marginal rates for most income levels and lowered the maximum marginal national income tax rate from 70 to 60 percent. Proposals by the Ministry of Finance made in 1988 would further reduce the marginal tax rates. These proposals would reduce the number of tax brackets from 12 to 5 and lower the tax rates to between 10 and 50 percent.[7]

While these marginal rates may seem high, relatively few people actually pay such high tax rates because of the many exemptions and deductions used in determining taxable income. Shoven examined the income tax threshold for a family of four composed of an employee, his spouse, and two children, one of whom is between 16 and 22 years old. The taxpayer receives a basic exemption (330,000 yen), an exemption for the spouse and each child (330,000 each), and deductions for employment income and social insurance premiums. Together, these deductions mean the individual could earn up to 2.6 million yen without incurring a tax liability. At the time of Shoven's analysis, average annual earnings in Japan were approximately 4 million yen. In 1987, this represented twice the tax threshold prevailing in the United States.[8]

Examining tax information for 1970, Pechman and Kaizuka found that 32 percent of the total income was not reported on tax returns in Japan or was reported by persons who were not taxable; the corresponding figure for the United States was 10 percent. As a result of the exemptions and deductions, the tax base in Japan amounted to only 33 percent of total income, compared to 59 percent in the United States.[9]

The tax liability for most types of income is determined by a taxpayer declaration. Taxes are then withheld from the payment of income. Due to this sophisticated withholding system, many individuals do not even have to file a tax return. There is no formal indexing for inflation, but tax cuts are typically made to compensate for the effects of inflation.

Corporate Income Taxes

The corporate tax on the income for firms is computed by multiplying taxable income of the corporation by the appropriate marginal tax rates. The corporate income tax in Japan is similar to that of the United States. The tax base is gross income minus gross expenses. Gross income includes revenue from sales of commodities and manufactured products, sales of fixed assets, interest, and other income. The tax rate is essentially flat except for differential treatment for very small firms. The primary difference between the Japanese and the U.S. corporate income tax is the Japanese treatment of dividends distributed to shareholders.

For companies with capital of more than 100 million yen, the tax rate on retained profits is 42 percent, and the tax rate of profits distributed as dividends is 32 percent. For companies with capital of 100 million yen or less, the tax on income of less than 8 million yen is 30 percent for retained profits and 24 percent for profits distributed as dividends. For income in excess of 8 million yen, the tax rates rise to 42 and 30 percent, respectively.

Prefectural governments also employ an enterprise, or corporate, income tax. The standard tax rates for corporations on ordinary taxable income are 6 percent if annual income is not more than 3.5 million yen, 9 percent if annual income is between 3.5 and 7 million yen, and 12 percent if annual income is in excess of 7 million yen. The reduced rates of 6 and 9 percent are not applicable to corporations with offices in more than three prefectures and capital of 10 million or more yen. The Ministry of Finance estimated that the overall marginal corporate income tax rate on equity income, including national and local taxes, was 51.6 percent in 1988.[10]

Since 1962, companies have been able to make tax-deductible contributions into tax-qualified pension plans, which are not counted as current income to their workers. Before the 1962 amendments to the Corporation Tax and Income Tax Laws, any pension contributions by a company to a trust bank or life insurance company were treated as an expense of the corporation but were subject to income tax as employee compensation at the time of the transfer. A similar tax status was awarded to employees' pension funds in 1966. A trust must be established for these pension funds.

The rules and regulations for both types of pension plans are examined in Chapter 5. Trust revenues and expenses are not counted as revenues or expenses of the pension plan sponsor. In addition, the revenues and expenses of the pension funds are not counted as revenues and expenses of the trust companies managing the pension plan. The taxable income of the trust company consists only of the amount received as trust fees. A tax of 1.173 percent per year is levied on the tax-qualified pension funds held by trust banks or life insurance companies; 1 percent is a national tax, and 0.173 percent is a local tax. This tax is considered interest on income tax not paid during the period of tax deferral. The accumulated sum of assets held by a company for its employees as part of an Employees' Assets Formation Plan also is subject to this 1 percent national tax. Assets in employees' pension funds are also subject to these taxes; however, there is a substantial deduction for these pension funds. This deduction is sufficiently large that relatively few employees' pension funds pay any tax.

Firms are not allowed to establish a tax-exempt reserve fund for their lump-sum severance pay systems. No special tax advantage is given to firms if they make contributions into a trusteed fund. Instead, a partial tax deduction is given when liabilities in these plans are accrued and noted in the form of a book reserve.

Tax Policy and the Growth of Pension Plans

This description of the Japanese tax structure indicates that there are considerable tax incentives for private savings in the tax code. Most individuals could have earned a tax-exempt return on most of their savings prior to 1987. These incentives represent a partial explanation for the high savings rate in Japan.

Since 1962, companies have been able to establish trusteed pension plans on behalf of their workers with contributions that are tax

TABLE 4–1 Coverage by Retirement Benefit Plans

Size of Firm (number of employees)	Percent of Firms with Retirement System	Percent of Firms with Retirement System Offering		
		Lump Sum Only	Annuity Only	Both
Total				
1975	90.7%	67.1%	13.2%	19.7%
1981	92.1	55.4	18.5	26.2
1985	89.0	51.9	14.3	33.8
1,000 or more				
1975	97.8	40.2	4.3	56.5
1981	99.6	24.6	11.5	63.9
1985	99.9	18.1	10.1	71.8
300–999				
1975	97.4	50.3	9.1	40.6
1981	99.4	36.2	20.6	43.2
1985	98.5	32.0	16.8	51.1
100–299				
1975	96.6	63.0	11.3	25.3
1981	95.9	49.2	22.2	28.6
1985	94.9	40.4	17.0	42.5
30–99				
1975	87.7	71.3	14.6	14.1
1981	90.0	60.3	17.3	22.4
1985	86.1	58.8	13.3	27.8

SOURCE: Ministry of Labor, *Taishoku-Kin Seido Sogo Chosa Hokoku,* as reported in Kiyoshi Murakami, "Retirement Benefits and Pension Plans in Japan," Sophia University Business Series Bulletin no. 118, 1988, p. 13.

deductible to the firm and not counted as current income to their workers. The same tax treatment is not given to the traditional lump-sum severance plans. This differential tax treatment is one of the major factors driving the current movement toward greater reliance on pension plans. For the most part, the current tax treatment of pension plans in Japan is similar to that in the United States. The primary exception is that in Japan the assets in pension funds are taxed.

COVERAGE BY RETIREMENT PLANS

In Japan, private retirement plans are either lump-sum severance payment plans or pension plans that provide annuity benefits. The pension plans often include options for lump-sum distributions instead of an annuity. One or both of these types of retirement plans are offered by 90 percent of all firms in Japan. Table 4–1 shows that virtually all employers with 300 or more workers provide some type of retirement plan for their regular workers. Smaller firms are less likely to offer retirement benefits; however, even among firms with between 30 and 99 workers, over 85 percent have at least one of these plans. These total coverage rates by some type of retirement plan are much higher than the pension coverage rate in the United States, which is estimated to be just over 50 percent.[11]

The coverage rates based on percent of firms with retirement plans in Japan probably overestimate the percentage of all workers covered by a retirement plan. This follows from the exclusion of part-time workers from participation in many company benefits, including pensions and lump-sum plans. In addition, the Japanese estimates are based on a survey limited to firms with at least 30 workers. This omission of very small firms, which are less likely to offer retirement plans, will tend to overestimate the proportion of workers actually covered by a retirement plan.

During the past decade, there does not appear to have been any trend in coverage by some type of retirement plan. However, an increasing proportion of firms now offer an annuity pension, and there has been a decline in the proportion of firms offering only a lump-sum plan. The average expenditure on retirement benefits by large firms in 1982 represented 4.9 percent of total labor costs.[12]

The traditional method of providing retirement income has been to grant lump-sum payments to retiring workers. Table 4–1 shows that the proportion of firms with some type of retirement plan offering only lump-sum severance payments has fallen from 67 percent in 1975 to 52 percent in 1985. This decline in firms with only lump-sum plans is especially prevalent among larger employers. Paralleling this trend is the increase in the proportion of firms with a pension annuity system. The percentage of firms with pension plans rose from 33 percent in 1975 to 48.1 percent in 1985. Among firms with 1,000 or more employees, 82 percent now have pension plans. Pensions are either tax-qualified pension plans, employees' pension funds, or non-qualified pension plans. The growth and development of pension plans is examined in the next chapter.

LUMP–SUM SEVERANCE PAY

Most Japanese companies provide severance pay in the form of a lump-sum benefit to workers leaving the firm. These payments are awarded to departing workers whether termination is employee or employer initiated. Benefits may be denied if the worker is fired for misconduct. The severance pay system was introduced in the 19th century and covered civil servants and employees in large firms. In 1935, 53 percent of all manufacturing firms with 100 or more employ-

TABLE 4–2 Average Voluntary Lump-Sum Benefits as Percent of Involuntary Benefits

Years of Service	Large Firms		Small Firms	
	1975	1985	1974	1986
1			52%	72%
3	50%		62	70
5	56	50%	66	72
10	67	60	74	78
15	75	69	79	81
20	84	78	83	84
25	89	82	86	87
30	91	87	88	87

SOURCE: Large-firm data is based on Central Labor Relations Commission, *Taishoku-Kin Teinen-Sei oyobi Nenkin Jijo Chosa*. Small-firm data is based on Tokyo Municipal Government, Labor Department, *Taishoku-Kin Jijo*. Data are reported in Kiyoshi Murakami, "Retirement Benefits and Pension Plans in Japan," Sophia University Business Series no. 118, 1988, p. 6.

ees offered a lump-sum severance plan. The government made these severance pay plans mandatory in 1936 as a substitute for introducing an unemployment insurance system. Mandatory lump-sum plans were abolished in the 1940s when the Employees' Pension Insurance system was introduced.[13] After World War II, lump-sum disbursements at the end of work life became an important retirement benefit for many workers.[14]

Qualifying for Benefits

While payments are made for both voluntary (worker-initiated) and involuntary (firm-initiated) retirement, the amount of the retirement allowance is lower for voluntary departures. The objective of penalties for early departure is to limit worker turnover. Table 4–2 shows that among large firms, the average ratio of voluntary retirement benefits to involuntary retirement benefits is only 50 percent if retirement (or quitting) occurs after only five years of service. This ratio rises to 87 percent for retirement after 30 years of service. The penalties for early departure from a large firm increased between 1975 and 1985. Smaller firms have less severe penalties on voluntary earlier departure, and these penalties have declined slightly.

A worker becomes eligible for a severance benefit from involuntary retirement within the first two years of service. Somewhat longer service is needed to qualify for a benefit if the departure is worker initiated. Smaller firms require a longer period of service to qualify for severance pay than do larger firms.[15] For example, Table 4–3 shows that 87 percent of large firms provide a lump-sum payment to

TABLE 4–3 Minimum Service Requirements for Eligibility for Lump-Sum Severance
Payment (percent of companies)

Years of Required Service	Large Companies (1985)		Small Companies (1986)	
	Voluntary	Involuntary	Voluntary	Involuntary
0–1	3.1%	48.7%	1.6%	17.3%
1–2	29.3	38.1	20.1	30.1
2–3	18.1	4.7	17.2	11.7
3 or more	49.5	8.5	50.6	23.8
Not available			10.6	17.1

SOURCE: Large-firm data is based on Central Labor Relations Commission, *Taishoku-Kin Teinen-Sei oyobi Nenkin Jijo Chosa*. Small-firm data is based on Tokyo Municipal Government, Labor Department, *Taishoku-Kin Jijo*. Data are reported in Kiyoshi Murakami, "Retirement Benefits and Pension Plans in Japan," Sophia University Business Series no. 118, 1988, p. 7.

workers who leave involuntarily after only two years of employment, while half of these firms require three or more years of service to qualify for a worker-initiated termination. Even among small firms, almost half provide benefits to workers who were involuntarily terminated after as little as two years of service.

These very short employment requirements to qualify for a lump-sum benefit differ substantially from the rather long vesting periods required for pension plans in Japan (see Chapter 5). Similar long vesting periods prevailed in the United States prior to the passage of the Employee Retirement Income Security Act (ERISA) in 1974. This legislation required U.S. firms to adopt one of several vesting standards, with most plans adopting a 10-year vesting rule. Recent legislation in the United States has lowered vesting to five years of service.

Calculation of Benefits

Lump-sum payments are calculated without regard to the departing employee's age, although reaching the age of mandatory retirement may be a factor in involuntary job termination. In general, the benefit formula is a function of the final month's basic salary and the number of years of service.[16] The formula usually increases with years of service, and benefits average about one month's final salary for each year of service. Within a company, the benefit formula is typically the same for all types of workers. Lump-sum retirement payments are a larger proportion of final salary among large employers.

In 1988, average lump-sum payments to male college graduates leaving at age 60 were equal to 3.5 years of annual salary. For a male high school graduate, lump-sum payments averaged 3.7 years of annual earnings.[17] The greater relative benefits paid to those with lower ed-

TABLE 4–4 Lump-Sum Retirement Allowance for Involuntary Termination, Large Firms

Years of Service	College Graduate		High School Graduate	
	Benefit (millions of yen)	Months of Final Pay	Benefit (millions of yen)	Months of Final Pay
5	0.6	3.1	0.5	3.3
10	2.0	7.2	1.5	7.1
15	4.3	12.4	3.2	12.4
20	8.2	19.1	5.9	19.4
25	13.7	27.2	9.7	27.1
30	20.2	35.4	14.4	35.0

SOURCE: Nippon Dantai Life Insurance Company, "Recent Studies on Severance and Retirement Benefit Plans," August 1988, pp. 6–7. The data is based on a survey by the Central Labor Relations Board in 1987 that covered firms with at least 1,000 employees.

ucational attainment is due to their greater job tenure at retirement.[18] Those with higher education will receive larger absolute benefits due to their higher average earnings.

The value of the retirement allowance paid by large firms is shown in Table 4–4. Although the table indicates benefits separately by educational attainment, there will be no differential treatment within any particular plan. The data indicate that the average college graduate who remains with a firm for 30 years would receive a lump-sum payment of 20.2 million yen ($140,000 at an exchange rate in 1987 of 144.6 yen per dollar), or approximately 3 years' salary. The payment for a high school graduate is about 30 percent lower. Higher benefits are achieved with longer service.

Reserve Funding

Firms establishing a reserve fund to pay lump-sum benefits can do so within the firm or with a public or financial institution outside the firm.

Typically, most employees establish a reserve fund that is, in effect, a book reserve. Rather than making contributions into an investment account from which future benefits are paid, most firms retain these funds in the company and create a liability on their books. As of March 31, 1989, tax-exempt book reserves totaled 10.9 trillion yen. The total amount of book reserves is considerably greater as only 40 percent of total reserves are tax deductible.[19]

These funds have been an important source of capital to many firms. In principle, the retirement allowance funds are used for investment in the company—making the employees partial owners of the company or, alternatively, creditors of the company by holding this implied debt.[20] In general, future payment of the lump sum is conditional on the continued survival of the firm. In most cases, workers whose employer goes bankrupt will not collect on the promised lump-sum benefit; however, a portion of the severance payment may be paid as part of Japan's system of workman's compensation insurance. This program insures workers against the nonpayment of compensation by firms in bankruptcy.

If an employer creates a book reserve account for these plans to provide for future benefits, the company receives a tax deduction equal to the least of:

1. 40 percent of the amount that would be payable at the end of the year if all employees voluntarily terminated, less the deduction allowed up to the end of the previous year.
2. The full amount payable at the end of the year if all employees voluntarily terminated, less the amount payable at the beginning of the year if all employees had voluntarily terminated.
3. 6 percent of total payroll.

However, no additional tax deduction is permitted if the company creates a fund for these retirement systems and invests those funds in assets outside the company. As a result of this tax treatment, most lump-sum plans are based solely on book reserves.

Lump-sum retirement payments are very popular in Japan. These benefits are used by retirees for a variety of purposes. A 1980 survey by the Ministry of Labor indicated that of persons retiring between 1972 and 1978 who received a lump-sum payment, 49 percent indicated some of these funds would be used for paying off housing loans or buying real estate. Thirty percent of retirees responded that the money would be used for the marriage of their children, and 11 percent stated that the funds would go to the education of their children. Sixty-one percent of the retirees indicated they would save some of the money for their remaining retirement years.[21]

Small Enterprise Retirement Allowance Mutual Aid Plan

Small firms sometimes entrust their severance pay plan to the Special Retirement Allowance Mutual Aid Scheme, which is administered by the local municipality, or to the Smaller Enterprise Retirement Allowance Mutual Aid Plan, which is managed by the government. The latter program was established in 1959 to encourage small firms to adopt retirement allowance plans. The government provides financial assistance to cover administrative costs and some funds to subsidize the retirement allowance.[22] The plan pays lump-sum retirement allowances to workers when they retire.

Firms with less than 300 regular employees may participate in this program. Employers make regular contributions of up to 20,000 yen per month.[23] There are no employee contributions. Contributions may be the same for all employees or vary with salary and length of service. One third of these contributions are subsidized by the government for two years for new participants. Employer contributions are tax deductible.

A lump-sum benefit is payable upon the termination of employment. The amount of the lump sum is determined by employer contributions and length of participation. On March 31, 1989, there were 343,257 employers participating in the Small Enterprise Retirement Allowance Plan covering 2.3 million employees. In fiscal 1987, average monthly contributions per employee were 5,368 yen and average payments were 523,305 yen. In March 1988, total assets in these plans were 1.3 trillion yen.

The benefits of workers who change jobs among employers participating in the Small Enterprise Retirement Allowance Plan are portable. Benefit credits accumulated with the new employer are simply added to those from the old employer. In practice, relatively few persons take advantage of this portability, choosing instead to accept a lump-sum distribution at the termination of employment. Only 2.8 percent of the 243,833 terminated employees in fiscal 1987 elected to retain their credits in the plan with the rest accepting lump-sum payments.[24]

CHANGING NATURE OF LUMP-SUM PLANS

The expenditures on severance pay plans have risen rapidly over the past 20 years due to wage increases and the increased number of workers at retirement age. Since these plans typically are not funded, firms faced the prospects of large annual payouts to support this system of retirement income. During this period, firms began to shift from lump-sum severance pay systems to pension plans (see Chapter 5). An important factor stimulating this trend was the establishment of favorable tax treatment accorded pensions beginning in 1962. More than 80 percent of firms with 1,000 or more employees have transformed their traditional retirement plans, partially or fully, into funded pensions. Since most retirees select lump-sum options offered by the pension plan, these changes may be more apparent than real.

A related development has been the tendency to slow down the rate of growth of basic salary for older workers. The Ministry of Labor has encouraged firms to limit the rising cost of retirement benefits by stopping automatic increases of basic salary after age 45 or 50. Firms have also attempted to slow down the rising cost of lump-sum payments by not counting years of service after age 55 in the calculation of the lump-sum payment.

Some firms have attempted to reduce the cost of an aging labor force by encouraging early retirement. In 1986, just over 4 percent of all firms with 30 or more employees offered early retirement with favorable treatment. Early retirement plans are much more prevalent among large firms, as over 50 percent of companies with 5,000 or more workers and 40 percent of companies with 1,000 to 4,999 employees offered early retirement incentives. By comparison, only 17 percent of firms with 300 to 999 employees have early retirement plans, and less than 6 percent of smaller firms offer these incentives.[25] These early retirement plans have been established even as the government has strongly encouraged firms to hire more older workers.

A final response to the rising cost of lump-sum retirement allowances has been to reduce the benefit formulas used to determine the lump-sum payment. Shamada summarizes this development by concluding that "in years when the number of workers who are old enough to receive retirement allowances was small, employers paid them relatively lavishly partly to encourage long-term commitments of workers, but in the years in which the number of eligible workers is large and increasing, employers begin to cut down the payment."[26] Formulas for lump-sum severance plans can be reduced by the firm. Thus, the security of these benefits to workers is limited by the lack of funding and by the potential downgrading of these benefits prior to retirement.

ENDNOTES

1. John Shoven, "The Japanese Tax Reform and the Effective Rate of Tax on Japanese Corporate Investments," National Bureau of Economic Research Working Paper no. 2791, December 1988, p. 3.

2. Ministry of Finance, An Outline of Japanese Taxes, 1988 (Tokyo: Japanese Government, 1988), p. 17.

3. This discussion is based on information from Ministry of Finance, Outline of Japanese Taxes, 1988.

4. For a detailed description of the items included in each of these types of income, see H. Homma, T. Maeda, and K. Hashimoto, "Japan," in *Comparative Tax Systems*, ed. Joseph Pechman (Arlington, Va.: Tax Analysts, 1987). This paper also examines the process of determining tax liability in Japan.

5. Shoven, "Japanese Tax Reform," pp. 8–10.

6. Atushi Nagono, "Japan," in *World Tax Reform: A Progress Report*, ed. Joseph Pechman (Washington, D.C.: The Brookings Institution, 1988), pp. 155–61.

7. Shoven, "Japanese Tax Reform."

8. Ibid., pp. 6–7.

9. Joseph Pechman and Keimei Kaizuka, "Taxation," in *Asia's New Giant: How the Japanese Economy Works*, ed. Hugh Patrick and Henry Rosovsky (Washington, D.C.: The Brookings Institution, 1976).

10. Shoven, "Japanese Tax Reform," p. 12.

11. Emily Andrews, *The Changing Profile of Pensions in America* (Washington, D.C.: Employee Benefit Research Institute, 1985).

12. Yoshitaka Fujita, *Employee Benefits and Industrial Relations* (Tokyo: Japan Institute of Labor), p. 30.

13. Kiyoshi Murakami, "Severance and Retirement Benefits in Japan," in *Pension Policy: An International Perspective*, ed. John Turner and Lorna Dailey (Washington, D.C.: U.S. Government Printing Office, forthcoming).

14. Yoshitaka Fujita, *Employee Benefits and Industrial Relations*.

15. Kiyoshi Murakami, "Retirement Benefits and Pension Plans in Japan," Sophia University Business Series no. 118, 1988, p. 7.

16. In Japan, employee compensation consists of a basic salary and various allowances. In some companies, the final monthly basic salary used to calculate retirement benefits is nearly 100 percent of total compensation or regular salary, while in other companies, it is much lower. Bonuses are always excluded from earnings used to calculate lump-sum severance payments. A recent study by the Central Labor Relations Commission found that the base salary is, on average, 55.5 percent of the regular salary. See Murakami, "Retirement Benefits and Pension Plans in Japan," p. 10.

17. International Benefit Information Service, April 1989, p. 14.

18. This follows from those with less education being hired at an earlier age. Thus, if they remain with the same company until retirement, they will have more years of service than college graduates.

19. Murakami, "Severance and Retirement Benefits in Japan," p. 26.

20. Fujita, *Employee Benefits and Industrial Relations*, pp. 35–36.

21. Survey conducted by Ministry of Labor, 1980. Data provided to me by Junichi Sakamoto, senior actuary, Pension Bureau, Ministry of Health and Welfare.

22. Japan Institute of Labor, *Wages and Hours of Work*, Japanese Industrial Relations Series no. 3, p. 18.

23. For firms in the wholesale sector, the maximum firm size is 100 and for the retail and service sectors, the maximum is 50 employees.

24. Murakami, "Severance and Retirement Benefits in Japan," pp. 22–23, 25.

25. Ministry of Labor, *Yearbook of Labour Statistics: 1986* (Tokyo: Japanese Government, 1987), p. 50.

26. Haruo Shimada, *The Japanese Employment System* (Tokyo: The Japan Institute of Labor, 1980), p. 17.

CHAPTER 5

_____Private Pension Plans_____

The development of private pensions in Japan was stimulated by legislation passed in the 1960s that granted preferential tax status to the funding of pensions. During the past 25 years, pension coverage has expanded throughout the Japanese economy. Pensions have become an increasingly important source of retirement income, especially among retirees from large firms.

In general, Japanese pension plans are either tax-qualified pension plans or employees' pension funds. Employees' pension funds are coordinated with the social security system. Employees' pension funds must accept responsibility for paying the earnings-related social security benefit and then must provide an additional or supplemental benefit. They can only be offered by large employers or groups of employers. Tax-qualified plans are more prevalent among smaller firms. These plans have lump-sum options, and almost all retirees select a lump-sum payment instead of an annuity. Tax-qualified plans are not coordinated with social security, and these plans do not allow the contracting out of any portion of social security.

The characteristics of these two types of pensions are examined in this chapter, along with a brief history of their development. This analysis will relate these systems to the aging of the population, changes in social security, and other emerging policy changes. Issues relating to benefit design, funding methods, and investment policy are reviewed and compared to prevailing policies in the United States.

TAX–QUALIFIED PENSIONS

Tax-qualified pension plans were introduced in 1962 with the amendments to the Corporation Tax Law and the Income Tax Law. These changes provided a favorable tax treatment for pension contributions and the reserve funds for tax-qualified pension plans meeting requirements specified in the 1962 laws. Specifically, employer contributions are treated as a business expense and, therefore, a deductible expense in calculation of corporate income tax liability. Neither these contributions nor plan earnings are considered current compensation to employees. When retirees receive a pension, these funds are treated as retirement income for personal income tax. In contrast to pensions in the United States, the assets in the reserve fund itself are taxed at a rate of 1.173 percent per year; 1 percent is a national tax, and 0.173 percent is a local tax.

These tax-qualified plans were designed on the model of defined benefit pensions in the United States. A company with 15 or more employees can establish a tax-qualified pension with the approval of the director general of the National Tax Administration, Ministry of Finance. All employees of the firm, except company directors, must be eligible to participate in the plan. These plans are not allowed to discriminate among employees with respect to coverage, qualifications for benefits, benefit formula, or contribution rates. Tax-qualified plans are managed by the sponsoring employer.

Benefit Determination

Benefits must be based on years of service using either a flat benefit or an earnings-related formula. Benefits are based on regular earnings, excluding overtime pay, bonuses, and contribution by the company to benefit plans. The benefit factor usually increases with respect to years of service up to 30 years of tenure. After 30 years of service, the increase in the pension benefit for continued work is often reduced. For example, benefits may be equal to 1 percent of final salary for each of the first 20 years of service plus 2 percent of salary for service between 20 and 30 years. For service after 30 years, the benefit formula would fall back to 1 percent. Credited service is typically defined as continuous service, although authorized absences are not held against the worker in determining benefits.

Benefits must be paid in the form of an annuity or a lump sum. Benefits are payable only on retirement or involuntary termination. The annuity may be a single life annuity without refund features, a single life annuity with certain payments, or payments for a fixed period of 5, 10, or 15 years. Most plans do not offer life annuity options.[1] In virtually all plans, the retiree can select a lump-sum payment in place of an annuity. The lump-sum conversion from the annuity uses an interest rate specified by the Ministry of Finance. For some time, this rate has been 5.5 percent. These plans rarely offer joint and survivor options when the benefit is taken as an annuity.

Workers who leave the firm prior to normal retirement receive a lump-sum payment as there is no practice of providing a vested deferred annuity. Benefits cannot be integrated with social security. Larger companies tend to set lower ages of eligibility for pensions than do smaller firms.

Tax Status of Benefits

Prior to 1988, pension benefits received as an annuity were taxed as salary income. A revision in the Income Tax Law in 1988 altered this tax treatment, and annuities are now taxed as miscellaneous income. In addition, the level of deductible pension income was raised. The minimum deduction for annual pension annuities received from a company pension plus social security benefits was increased in 1989; retirement annuities are now tax free up to 2.9 million yen ($22,304 at an exchange rate of 128.5 yen per dollar, which prevailed in the first quarter of 1989) for a couple age 65 and older, and 1.8 million yen ($14,008) for a couple younger than 65. For single persons age 65 and older, the tax-exempt amount is 2.1 million yen ($15,953), and for a single person younger than age 65, 0.95 million yen ($7,393). A detailed review of deductions in 1988 for annuities is provided in Chapter 4.

Tax-qualified pensions were established to permit the payment of retirement annuities from pension funds accumulated using tax-deferred contributions. However, given the availability of the lump-sum option, these plans have become, in practice, a means of funding lump-sum payments. Of the total benefits paid through tax-qualified pensions from April 1987 to March 1988, only 10 percent were in the form of annuity payments, while 90 percent were in lump-sum settlements.[2] To encourage more workers to accept annuities, some firms are offering a greater present value in the form of annuities than as a lump sum. Some firms are beginning to allow employees to select part of their pension as an annuity and part as a lump sum.[3]

The decision to select a lump-sum distribution depends on the tax treatment of the two payments, the interest rate used to convert annuity payments into a lump-sum payment, and inflationary expectations. The 5.5 percent interest rate used for conversion is greater than the yield on government bonds that has prevailed since 1986; bond yields ranged from 3.6 to 5.2 percent during this period.[4] A higher-than-market interest rate lowers the lump-sum value and should tend to discourage retirees' use of lump-sum payments. The low and stable rates of inflation that characterized the Japanese economy in the 1980s should make fixed annuity payments more appealing.[5] Despite the advantages of selecting an annuity option, retirees overwhelmingly continue to select lump-sum distributions.

Financing of Pensions

Employer contributions to a tax-qualified plan must be either a specified dollar amount or a specified percentage of payroll. Contributions are determined using a reasonable actuarial method to determine liabilities. Past service liability must be amortized according to one of three approved methods: a flat amount of unfunded liabilities, a certain percentage of total earnings, and a certain percentage of un-amortized liabilities at the end of the previous year. Employee contributions are typically not required in tax-qualified pensions, with one estimate showing that only 2 percent of the plans required employee contributions in 1980.[6]

Liabilities are determined using service-to-date and a projection of future earnings. The earnings projection is based on the tenure–earnings relationship prevailing in the company at that time. Future earnings growth due to inflation and productivity increases is ignored in the calculation of liabilities. Liabilities are calculated using an interest rate set by the Ministry of Finance. For some time, this rate has been 5.5 percent. Funding is limited to 100 percent of these liabilities.

In general, the Japanese view the assets of the pension fund as belonging to the participants of the plan. Thus, in the case of termination, the plan assets are divided among current workers and retirees. Tax-qualified pension plans must be actuarially evaluated at least every five years. At the time of the review, all excess reserves must be returned to the employer. Excess reserves cannot be recaptured by the employer at any other time. Given the withdrawal of excess funds at each review, it seems more appropriate to view these pension funds as an irrevocable trust, with the liability being what is necessary to pay currently promised benefits. Since excess funds can be removed at the time of an actuarial review, we would expect firms to remove all excess funds prior to any termination of the plan.

These techniques imply that plans will be underfunded on an ongoing basis, as firms are not allowed to make contributions to fund expected future salary increases due to real productivity growth. For

TABLE 5-1 Number of Tax-Qualified Pension Plans*

Year	Firm Size (number of employees)				Total
	15-99	*100-299*	*300-999*	*1,000+*	*Total*
1980	48,724	8,077	2,261	420	59,482
1983	51,598	9,198	2,592	620	64,008
1985	53,116	10,098	2,911	716	66,841
1986	53,933	10,520	3,050	765	68,268
1987	56,352	10,857	3,186	808	71,203
1988	59,099	11,173	3,298	853	74,423
1989	62,552	11,622	3,502	879	78,555

*All data are for March of the indicated year. Prior to 1986, minimum firm size in survey was 20.

SOURCE: 1980–87 data are reported in Kiyoshi Murakami, "Retirement Benefits and Pension Plans in Japan," Sophia University Business Series Bulletin no. 118, 1988, p. 14. 1988 data are reported in Nippon Dantai Life Insurance Company, *Recent Studies on Severance and Retirement Benefit Plans,* August 1988, p. 8.

the most part, firms are limited to funding at a termination value of pension liabilities. By comparison, firms in the United States are allowed to continue to make tax-exempt contributions as long as the fund is less than 150 percent of its termination liability. If the fund exceeds this limit, no new tax-exempt contributions can be made, but there is no requirement that excess funds be removed. In the United States, liabilities are determined using the average 30-year Treasury bond rate for the last four years.

Growth of Coverage

In 1966, four years after tax-qualified pensions were first allowed, only 8,150 such plans were in existence. These plans spread throughout the Japanese economy during the following two decades. Table 5–1 shows that the number of tax-qualified plans has increased in the 1980s from 59,482 in 1980 to 78,555 in 1989. Eighty percent of these plans are operated by firms with fewer than 100 employees. The number of participants in tax-qualified pension plans increased from 5.4 million in 1980 to 8.5 million in 1989.

Plan assets must be administered by either a trust bank, an insurance company, or the National Mutual Insurance Federation of Agricultural Cooperatives (Zenkyoren). At least 100 employees are necessary for the plan to be operated by a trust bank. Life insurance companies can manage plans with as few as 15 employees. Authority to manage tax-qualified pension plan assets was granted to Zenkyoren in 1982. Currently, these agricultural cooperatives manage less than 1 percent of plan assets. Given the size distribution of plans, it is not surprising that most tax-qualified pension plans are managed by life

TABLE 5–2 Tax-Qualified Pension Funds Invested in Insurance Companies and Trust Banks

As of March 31	Insurance Companies (million yen)	Trust Banks (million yen)
1976	454,658	585,445
1977	563,295	751,544
1978	700,121	932,687
1979	872,334	1,135,853
1980	1,101,268	1,377,137
1981	1,384,523	1,667,766
1982	1,722,477	1,984,133
1983	2,120,019	2,335,607
1984	2,582,538	2,694,631
1985	3,311,702	3,087,644
1986	3,688,095	3,499,534
1987	4,297,261	3,959,950
1988	4,975,113	4,456,588
1989	5,549,280	4,909,897

SOURCE: Ministry of Finance, Tax Bureau, *Tekikaku Taishoku Nenkin no Shojin Jokyo Shirabe*, as reported in Kiyoshi Murakami, "Retirement Benefits and Pension Plans in Japan," Sophia University Business Series Bulletin no. 118, 1988, p. 15. Data for 1988–1989 are from unpublished materials supplied by Kiyoshi Murakami.

insurance companies. Of the 74,423 plans operating in 1988, 66,891 are operated by insurance companies and 7,532 by trust banks.

Assets in tax-qualified pensions totaled 10.5 trillion yen in 1989 ($75.8 billion at an exchange rate of 138 yen per dollar), almost equally divided between plans operated by insurance companies and those operated by trust banks (see Table 5–2).

EMPLOYEES' PENSION FUNDS

The employees' pension fund system was established with the amendment of the Employees' Pension Insurance Law in 1965. Beginning in October 1966, employers could establish an employees' pension fund after having the plan approved by the Ministry of Health and Welfare. To establish an employees' pension fund, a firm must have 500 or more employees for a single-employer plan or 3,000 or more for a multiplan, and the plan must receive the approval of company unions. The minimum number of employees required for adoption of an employees' pension fund was initially 1,000 for a single-employer plan and 5,000 for a multiemployer plan. To encourage greater use of these plans, the minimum plan size has been lowered. As of March 1989, there were 1,259 employees' pension funds.

In addition to this size requirement, the Ministry of Health and Welfare only approves the establishment of an employees' pension

TABLE 5–3 Size Distribution of Employees' Pension Funds (March 1988)

		Single-Company and Allied Company	Multicompany	Total
Less than	2,000 members	349	1	350
	2,000– 2,999	165	12	177
	3,000– 3,999	104	29	133
	4,000– 4,999	55	42	97
	5,000– 9,999	112	141	253
	10,000–19,999	48	77	125
	20,000–29,999	12	15	27
	30,000 or more	15	17	32
	Total	860*	334	1,194

*These plans were divided into 405 single-company funds and 455 allied company funds.

SOURCE: Pension Fund Association, *Corporate Pension Plans in Japan* (Tokyo: 1989), p. 17.

fund by firms that are earning profits. Specifically, the sponsoring firm must not have incurred losses in any of the last three years. The Ministry also must approve the design of the plan and all funding requirements.

Distribution of Funds

Plans may cover workers in a single company, workers in two or more allied companies, or workers in two or more companies in the same industry or occupation. Revisions to regulations adopted in 1989 liberalized the rules concerning multiemployer plans to permit a plan to cover firms not in the same industry. Table 5–3 indicates the distribution of plans and workers covered by employees' pension funds by plan type and size of employer. Single-company plans plus employees' pension funds with allied companies account for 72 percent of all employees' pension funds. In March 1989, there were 421 single-company plans, covering 1.7 million workers. In addition, there were 2.6 million persons in 480 allied-company employees' pension funds and 4.0 million participants in 358 multiemployer plans.

Due to these governmental requirements, employees' pension funds tend to be larger than tax-qualified pension plans. The size distribution of employees' pension funds in Table 5–3 indicates the existence of a number of very large pension plans. For example, 15 percent of all the employees' pension funds have 10,000 or more members. Table 5–4 shows the distribution of plans across industries. The largest number of employees' pension funds are in the wholesale and retail trade sector, followed by machine manufacturing and finance. In March 1989, there were 8.3 million participants in employ-

TABLE 5–4 Industrial Distribution of Employees' Pension Funds (March 1988)

Industry	Number of Funds
Fishery	3
Construction	73
Food manufacturing	57
Textile manufacturing	60
Wooden goods manufacturing	10
Chemical	66
Metalworking	41
Machine	213
Other manufacturing	66
Wholesale and retail trade	249
Finance	139
Transportation and communication	90
Services	125
Electricity–gas–water	2
Total	1,194

SOURCE: Pension Fund Association, *Corporate Pension Plans in Japan* (Tokyo: 1989), p. 17.

ees' pension funds (up from 7.6 million in 1988), and these plans had assets totaling 19.4 trillion yen in 1989.

Employer contributions to these funds are treated as business expenses and are deductible from corporate income tax. Employee contributions to employees' pension funds are completely exempt from income tax in the same manner as are the contributions for social insurance programs.

Fund earnings are not subject to personal or corporate income tax; however, there is a 1 percent national tax and a 0.173 percent local tax on the fund itself above a specified minimum level of assets. The exemption of some plan assets from this tax was instituted so the combined Employees' Pension Insurance and employees' pension fund contributions would have the same tax status as the benefits in the public mutual aid associations. When the exemption was introduced, the employees' pension funds had to provide a supplemental benefit equal to 2.7 times the contracted-out benefit to equal the benefits to public workers. Thus, the exemption allows funds to accumulate assets to support benefits at this level without being subject to the tax on fund assets. This deduction results in the funds of most employees' pension funds being tax exempt.[7]

Benefit Determination

Employees' pension fund benefits are composed of two components. The substitutional component is directly linked to the national social security system. The social security benefit is composed of two parts: a flat benefit from the National Pension paid to everyone and an earnings component based on years of work and earnings throughout one's work life from the Employees' Pension Insurance system (see Chapter 3). In exchange for lower total social security contributions, the employees' pension fund assumes responsibility for paying the Employees' Pension Insurance benefit based on past earnings. In October 1988, the regular social security contribution rate was 12.4 percent for men and 11.75 percent for women, shared equally by the employer and the employee.[8] Adopting an employees' pension fund lowers social security contribution rates to 9.2 percent for men and 8.75 percent for women. These funds support the basic (flat) social security benefit for the worker and his spouse. The difference between the regular social security contribution rate and the rate for participants in employees' pension funds goes to finance the earnings-related, contracted-out benefit, which is now paid by the employees' pension fund. Contributions to pay the substitutional component of an employees' pension fund are shared equally by the worker and the firm.

In addition to this contracted-out benefit associated with social security benefits, employees' pension funds must include a supplementary component. The supplementary component must be not less than 30 percent of the substitutional Employees' Pension Insurance benefit accrued while working for this firm. Employer contributions to support this supplementary component must be at least equal to those required of employees. Any additional contributions to fund past service liabilities are typically paid by the employer. The supplemental benefit is in the form of a life annuity, and retirees are not allowed to select a joint and survivorship option.

Retirement income for retired employees consists of the basic benefit from the National Pension Plan, plus the contracted-out, earnings-related benefit paid the employees' pension fund, plus the supplemental pension benefit. In Chapter 3, the combined social security benefit under the new social security benefit formulas for a married worker with average earnings of 254,000 yen per month was shown to be 176,200 yen per month (see Figure 3–1). This represented a replacement rate of 69 percent. Adding the minimum allowed supplemental benefit of 30 percent of the contracted-out benefit raises the total retirement benefit to 199,060 yen, or a replacement rate of 78 percent of earnings. This calculation overestimates the replacement rate since the social security benefit is based on indexed past earnings while the supplemental pension benefit is based on unindexed salary average.

The supplemental benefit may be determined by one of three formulas. First, plans may provide the contracted-out portion of the social security benefit plus the supplemental benefit, which must be at least 30 percent of the substituted benefit. In these plans, the combined benefit from the employees' pension fund is based on a benefit formula of

$$B = (.0075) (1 + \alpha) \times \text{Average Salary} \times \text{Years Coverage}$$

In this formula, .0075 is the benefit for the contracted-out benefit and α is the supplemental benefit.

Within a plan, everyone is covered by the same formula; however, the size of the supplemental benefit varies across plans. The benefit formula is typically based on career earnings like the Employees' Pension Insurance benefit, which is being contracted out. Many plans using this benefit formula offer a lump-sum option on the supplemental benefit. The conversion to a lump sum is based on an interest rate set by the Ministry of Finance, currently 5.5 percent. The worker cannot convert the substitute benefit into a lump sum.

A second benefit formula followed from the process of phasing out existing lump-sum severance pay plans. Employers started employees' pension funds and set the benefit formula to hold total pension costs constant. In these plans, the contracted-out benefit is based on indexed career earnings, but the supplemental benefit is often based on a shorter averaging period. Plans offering this type of benefit also offer lump-sum options on the supplemental benefit.

The final type of formula, a final salary benefit, is used only in government-related corporations. There were only 13 plans of this type operating in 1988. These plans do not offer lump-sum options.

In 1973, an automatic cost-of-living adjustment was introduced for social security. The government takes the responsibility for paying postretirement increases on the substitute portion of the employees' pension fund benefit. Rarely do employees' pension funds award inflationary increases for the supplemental component of the retirement benefit.

Vesting of Benefits

After one month of employment the worker is fully vested in the contracted-out benefit. Vesting standards for the supplemental benefit are set by the Ministry of Health and Welfare. Currently, vesting for an annuity benefit generally occurs after 20 years of service for all employees' pension funds. The Pension Fund Association is a special judicial person established in 1966 under the provisions of the Employees' Pension Insurance Law. All employees' pension funds are required to be members of the Pension Fund Association. When workers leave firms prior to retirement, assets sufficient to pay the contracted-out benefit are transferred from the specific employees' pension fund to the Pension Fund Association.

The Pension Fund Association assumes the responsibility of the employees' pension fund for paying the contracted-out benefit to workers who leave firms with less than 10 years of service. Thus, the Pension Fund Association serves as a portability center for the contracted-out portion of the pension benefit. In 1987, the Pension Fund Association was paying benefits to 351,000 pensioners who had left their jobs prior to retirement.[9] No participant of an employees' pension fund can voluntarily withdraw from the fund unless his employment is terminated.

Actual vesting standards for the supplemental benefit vary among employees' pension funds; however, the typical plan provides no supplemental benefit to workers who leave with less than three years of insured coverage. Persons with 3 to 20 years of service will receive a traditional lump-sum severance benefit at termination, while retirees with 20 or more years of service are paid a pension annuity.[10]

In summary, a worker who leaves a firm and its employees' pension fund will have his future contracted-out benefit paid by the Pension Fund Association. If the worker receives an additional lump-sum settlement from the employees' pension fund, he has the option of transferring that amount to the Pension Fund Association. The association provides the worker with a life annuity that is actuarially equivalent to the lump sum.[11]

Plan Funding and Administration

Plan funding and administration are supervised by the Ministry of Health and Welfare. Permissible funding methods are the general average premium method and the entry age normal method. Funding requirements are based on acceptable actuarial assumptions as specified by the government. These include an assumed interest rate of 5.5 percent, the same mortality assumptions used for social security, and other needed assumptions based on recent plan experience.[12]

Funds are held and invested by either trust banks or insurance companies, although consideration is now being given to allowing the use of investment advisors and in-house investment management. The proposal under review would allow 127 investment management companies to manage new investments of employees' pension funds. Existing assets must continue to be managed by trust banks and insurance companies. A maximum of one third of plan assets could be managed by an investment company. To be eligible to use investment companies, the employees' pension fund must have been operating for at least eight years. In addition, employees' pension funds that are at least eight years old and have 50 billion yen in assets can manage up to one third of these funds in-house.[13]

A certified pension actuary is responsible for the financial management of employees' pension funds. The actuary confirms and signs all pension actuarial reports that the fund submits to the Ministry of Health and Welfare. He is also responsible for the settlement of the fund accounts and issues relating to benefit design. Certified pension actuaries must be approved by the Ministry of Health and Welfare.[14]

Past service liabilities recognized at the initiation of the plan or incurred in subsequent years should be amortized within 7 to 20 years. Liabilities are determined by projecting earnings out to retirement based on the current tenure–earnings relationship in the company. Future increases due to inflation and productivity increases are ignored. Funding is limited to 100 percent of these liabilities. An actuarial review of the plan must be conducted at least every five years.

The government determines permissible forms of investments and limits the composition of the portfolio. Fifty percent of the fund must be invested in capital-secured investments (government bonds, government-secured bonds, etc.). At most, 30 percent of the fund can be in stocks, 30 percent in foreign investments, and 20 percent in real estate. Finally, no more than 10 percent of the pension fund can be invested in the sponsoring company. This latter restriction is the same as that used in the United States. This same standard is applied to the investments of tax-qualified pension plans.

Employees' pension funds are organized as public corporations and established by employers and employees. A majority of employees and unions must approve the establishment of an employees' pension fund. The organizational structure includes a representative decision-making body consisting of an equal number of members appointed by employers and employees. These groups usually range from 14 to 68 members. The employees' pension fund also has a board of directors evenly divided between employer and employee representatives. The president of this board is selected from employer directors.[15] While formally these boards must approve various decisions by the fund, in practice they seem to have relatively little actual authority.

Employees' pension funds are not allowed to transfer excess assets from the fund to the sponsoring firm. Plans that are overfunded can consider reducing employer contributions or improving plan benefits. These changes must be approved by the Ministry of Health and Welfare. The Ministry reviews funds annually and may make recommendations for plan changes. Funds may request reductions in the benefit formulas to reduce financial liabilities. Any such changes must be approved by the Ministry. To date, no such requests have been approved.

In May 1988, the Diet passed legislation allowing the Pension Fund Association to be entrusted with some of the administrative responsibilities of small employees' pension funds. Individual funds may transfer to the Pension Fund Association such activities as recordkeeping and benefit payments. Centralizing these activities in the Pension Fund Association is expected to reduce the cost of managing small funds. This change in fund management was part of legislation to encourage the spread of pensions in the Japanese economy.

Termination of Funds

If an employees' pension fund terminates, assets equal to the actuarial present value of benefits of the substitutional component are taken by the government, which then reassumes the responsibility of paying this benefit. The government assumes responsibility for this benefit if assets are not sufficient to pay the substitute benefit.

Prior to 1989, the residual assets of terminating funds were divided among pensioners and current workers according to their pension credits. Firms were not responsible for any unfunded past service liabilities at termination. When a plan was terminated, retirees had their benefits stopped and were given a cash settlement. The sponsoring firm had to receive approval from the Ministry of Health and Welfare before an employees' pension fund could be terminated. Such permission was rarely given to ongoing firms. As of mid-1988, only 18 employee pension funds had been terminated.

Between 1966 and 1973, there were no employees' pension fund terminations; however, six plans were merged into existing plans during this period. Between 1974 and 1977, 6 plans were terminated, and between 1980 and 1985, another 12 plans were terminated. From the mid-1970s to the mid-1980s, 10 additional plans were merged with other funds.[16] In summary, employees' pension funds have been relatively stable since this pension system was established in 1966. This stability reflects the steady economic growth in Japan and the fact

TABLE 5–5 Trend in Number of Employees' Pension Funds: Starts, Mergers, and Terminations

Year	Total EPFs	New Funds Started	Merger	Terminations
1966	142	142	—	—
1967	305	163	—	—
1968	453	150	2	—
1969	581	128	—	—
1970	713	134	2	—
1971	811	98	—	—
1972	853	44	2	—
1973	892	39	—	—
1974	917	26	—	1
1975	929	14	—	2
1976	938	12	1	2
1977	945	9	1	1
1978	957	12	—	—
1979	983	26	—	—
1980	991	12	—	4
1981	1,008	20	1	2
1982	1,026	19	1	1
1983	1,043	22	4	—
1984	1,063	23	1	2
1985	1,073	32	1	3
1986	1,134	N/A	N/A	0
1987	1,194	N/A	N/A	0

SOURCE: Employees' Pension Fund Association, "Proposal of a Statutory System of Qualified Pension Actuary," April 1986, p. 52; and Katsuyuki Nonoshita and Junichi Sakamoto, "Introduction of the Pension Benefit Guaranty System in Japan," unpublished paper, August 1989.

that employees' pension funds are adopted only by larger successful firms. This pattern of development is shown in Table 5–5.

In mid-1988, the Diet passed pension legislation authorizing the establishment of a pension benefit guaranty system for employees' pension funds. Details of this system were to develop within a year so that the insurance scheme could be in place by mid-1989. This benefit guaranty system applies only to employees' pension funds and does not cover tax-qualified pension plans. The legislation established a system that if an employees' pension fund is terminated as a result of bankruptcy of the sponsoring firm, the Pension Fund Association will guarantee the payment of a certain amount of the supplementary benefit. In addition, the Pension Fund Association will pay the contracted-out substitute benefit.

After a year of negotiations, a pension guaranty system was initiated on April 1, 1989. The system guarantees the payment of a specified part of the supplementary benefit promised by the employees'

FIGURE 5–1 Amount of Guaranteed Pension Payment to Terminated Employees' Pension Funds

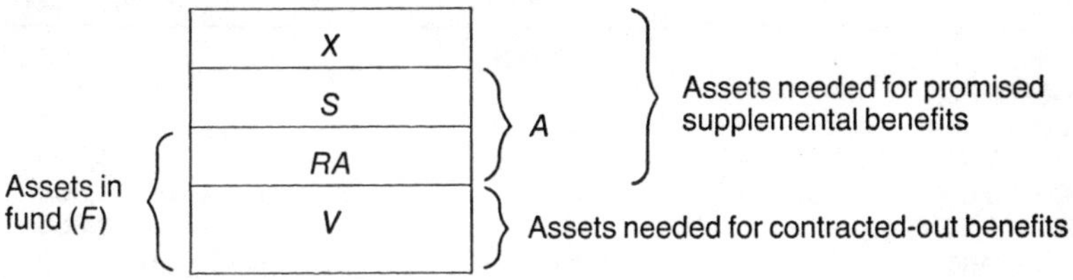

Amount of pension guaranty

$S = V \times [1 + A] - F$

Benefits promised but not guaranteed by system – X.
Fund reserves available to pay supplemental benefit – RA.

pension fund. The system is managed by the Pension Fund Association and supervised by the newly established Premium Payment Guaranty Project Steering Committee.

The committee will determine whether a termination of an employees' pension fund meets prescribed guidelines that qualify funds for the guaranty. Reasons for fund termination include bankruptcy of sponsoring employer, deterioration of the performance of the sponsoring firm, and unanticipated market conditions that make it difficult for the firm to maintain the fund.

The aggregate pension guaranty to a fund is a function of plan assets and the benefit that has been promised. The amount of the guaranty to a fund is shown in Figure 5–1 and determined by

$$\text{Guaranteed payment } (S) = V \times [1 + A] - F$$

where V is the minimum reserve fund necessary to pay the contracted-out benefit, A is the reserve needed to pay the supplemental benefit based on the fund's benefit formula (limited to 30 percent of V), and F is the amount of reserves in the fund. Therefore, S represents the amount of additional funds in excess of those currently held by the fund guaranteed to the terminating employees' pension fund. The guaranteed funds are sufficient to allow the Pension Fund Association to pay the substitute benefit and a supplemental benefit equal to 30 percent of the substitute benefit.

TABLE 5-6 Annual Contributions to Pension Guaranty System

Number of Participants	Contribution per Participant	Maximum Total Contribution (000s)
Less than 3,000	90 yen	255 yen
3,000– 5,000	85	400
5,000–10,000	80	750
10,000–15,000	75	1,050
15,000–20,000	70	1,300
20,000–30,000	65	1,800
30,000 or more	60	3,000

SOURCE: Katsuyuki Nonoshita and Junichi Sakamoto, "Introduction of the Pension Benefit Guaranty System in Japan," unpublished paper, August 1989, p. 19.

To support this system, employees' pension funds are required to pay a contribution that is a function of the number of participants in the fund. The annual contribution equals the number of participants times a unit contribution. As shown in Table 5–6, the unit contribution declines with plan size. For firms with less than 3,000 participants, the contribution is 90 yen per participant ($.70 at a first-quarter 1989 exchange rate of 128.5 yen per dollar), subject to a maximum contribution of 255,000 yen ($1,984). For funds with 30,000 or more participants, the contribution is 60 yen per participant ($.47), subject to a maximum of 3 million yen per year ($23,346).

The contribution is paid semiannually in May and November. Total premiums are estimated to be 619 million yen for fiscal 1989. The system is to be actuarially evaluated every five years, at which time premiums may be changed.[17]

The contributions are not required by law; however, during the first year of operation all plans contributed to the system. If the fund does not pay the contributions despite reminders by the president of the Pension Fund Association, the amount of the guaranteed payment will be reduced if the fund is terminated. The reliance on voluntary participation in the pension guaranty program differs sharply from the legally required contributions in the United States. The extent of continued participation by employees' pension funds remains to be determined.

NONQUALIFIED PRIVATE PENSIONS

The first corporate pension plans appeared in some industries at the end of the 1950s prior to any legislation providing preferential tax treatment. Some companies retained these plans even though legislation enacted in the 1960s provided favored tax treatment for approved pensions. Nonqualified, or unapproved, pension plans do not exist widely in Japan. These plans are primarily in large, tax-exempt companies and usually not funded. They are not subject to government regulation.

Benefits from these plans are taxed when received by retirees if the plans are unfunded. If funded, the employer's contribution must be treated as taxable income to someone. When the contribution is fully vested in an employee, the employer's contribution is deductible as a business expense to the firm but is taxable to the employee as current compensation. When the contribution is not vested in an employee, the employer's contribution cannot be deducted as a business expense, but it is not taxable to the employee. The contribution remains a part of company assets.

COMPARING EMPLOYEES' PENSION FUNDS AND TAX–QUALIFIED PENSIONS

Since the mid-1960s, pensions have spread throughout the Japanese economy. Table 5–7 shows that the number of employees' pension funds increased from 142 in 1967 to 1,259 in 1989. During this period, the number of covered workers rose from .5 million to 8.3 million. Similar growth is observed for tax-qualified pension plans, which covered 8.5 million workers in 1989. In March 1989, 16.7 million workers were covered by an employer pension. This represented 58.1 percent of workers covered by the earnings component of the social security system, the Employees' Pension Insurance system. This ratio has risen from 42.1 percent in 1977 and 45.3 percent in 1980 to its current level of 58.1 percent.[18]

The incidence of pension coverage is greater among large firms. This is shown by the high coverage rate among Japan's largest corporations. Eighty-seven percent of the 1,895 companies listed on the Tokyo Stock Exchange in September 1988 offered either a tax-qualified pension or an employees' pension fund. Employees' pension funds were more common among these major corporations (see Table 5–8).[19]

Although both plan types offer the option of retirement annuity income, there are substantial differences in these pensions. They are overseen by different governmental agencies: employees' pension funds by the Ministry of Health and Welfare, tax-qualified plans by the Ministry of Finance. Companies with as few as 15 workers can organize a tax-qualified pension, while only companies or multi-employer groups with over 500 workers can establish an employees'

TABLE 5-7 Participants in Employees' Pension Funds and Tax-Qualified Plans

Year (March 31)	Employees' Pension Funds		Tax-Qualified Pension Plans		Total Participants* (millions)	Workers Insured by EPI	Percentage of EPI-Insured Workers in Private Pension Plans
	Plans	Participants (millions)	Plans	Participants (millions)			
1967	142	0.50	16,224	1.51	2.01	19.19	10.5%
1972	811	4.67	64,747	3.83	8.50	22.51	37.8
1977	938	5.40	57,011	4.64	10.04	23.85	42.1
1978	945	5.44	57,001	4.91	10.35	23.90	43.3
1979	957	5.57	57,786	5.11	10.68	24.18	44.2
1980	983	5.79	59,482	5.41	11.20	24.71	45.3
1981	991	5.97	61,437	5.84	11.81	25.24	46.8
1982	1,008	6.18	62,775	6.26	12.44	25.70	48.4
1983	1,026	6.34	64,008	6.49	12.83	26.03	49.3
1984	1,043	6.56	65,346	6.87	13.43	26.36	50.9
1985	1,063	6.79	66,841	7.24	14.03	26.76	52.5
1986	1,073	7.06	68,268	7.56	14.60	27.07	54.2
1987	1,134	7.26	71,203	7.88	15.15	26.99	56.1
1988	1,194	7.64	74,423	8.21	15.85	27.68	57.3
1989	1,259	8.27	78,555	8.45	16.72	28.77	58.1

*Some of the members of the employees' pension funds and tax-qualified pensions are counted twice because some companies offer both types of plans.

SOURCE: Pension Fund Association, *Corporate Pension Plans in Japan* (Tokyo: 1989), p. 20. Data for 1989 are reported in Yoshiro Yumiba, "Private Pension Statistics in Japan," in *Pension Policy: An International Perspective*, ed. John Turner and Lorna Dailey (Washington, D.C.: U.S. Government Printing Office, forthcoming).

TABLE 5–8 Pension Coverage among Firms Listed on Japanese Stock Exchange

Date	Number of Companies Listed in Stock Exchanges	Number of Companies Adopting One or Both of the Plans	Percentage of Listed Companies with Pension	Type of Pensions		
				EPF	TQP	Both Plans
Dec. 1975	1,668	1,002	60.1%	365	585	52
Sept. 1978	1,657	1,039	62.7	383	599	57
Sept. 1979	1,674	1,130	67.5	387	675	68
Sept. 1980	1,682	1,170	69.6	391	708	78
Sept. 1981	1,697	1,279	75.4	787	391	101
Sept. 1982	1,716	1,320	76.9	828	376	116
Sept. 1983	1,735	1,365	78.7	861	379	125
Sept. 1984	1,748	1,420	81.2	906	373	141
Sept. 1985	1,778	1,475	83.0	957	361	157
Sept. 1986	1,806	1,511	83.7	990	354	167
Sept. 1987	1,851	1,594	86.1	1,040	374	180
Sept. 1988	1,895	1,649	87.0	1,075	378	196

SOURCE: Mitsubishi Trust and Banking Corporation, "Mitsubishi's Pension Bulletin," as reported in Pension Fund Association, *Corporate Pension Plans in Japan* (Tokyo: 1989), p. 21.

pension fund. To establish an employees' pension fund, workers must be covered by the employee component of social security, the Employees' Pension Insurance system.

In 1987, employees' pension funds paid 1.14 million beneficiaries an average annual pension of 257,000 yen ($1,777 at an exchange rate of 144.6 yen per dollar). The increase in the number of beneficiaries and average pension is shown in Table 5–9. Tax-qualified plans pay large benefits to fewer beneficiaries. The lower number of beneficiaries is due to the selection of lump-sum settlements by most participants in these plans. The higher average benefit is the result of employees' pension funds paying life annuities, while tax-qualified plans generally allow a fixed number of benefit payments.

Lump-sum options are available with both plan types, and most retirees select a lump-sum payment. A 1985 survey by the Central Labor Relations Board of 226 employers with 1,000 or more workers who have pension plans found that 213 offered lump-sum options. In 42 percent of the firms, 100 percent of employees opted for a lump-sum payment. In another 19 percent of the firms, 80 to 100 percent of employees selected lump-sum payments. This study included both tax-qualified plans and employees' pension funds.[20] The acceptance of lump-sum payments is much more prevalent among tax-qualified pension participants. The Pension Fund Association reported that in 1984, 53 percent of employees' pension fund participants selected annuity options, while only 2 percent of tax-qualified pension participants chose such options.[21]

TABLE 5–9 Number of Beneficiaries and Average Benefit Amounts*

| Year (March 31) | Employees' Pension Funds | | Tax-Qualified Plans | |
	Number of Pensioners (000s)	Annual Average Benefit	Number of Pensioners (000s)	Annual Average Benefit
1976	269	48,361 yen	32	159,973 yen
1977	324	57,647	35	164,525
1978	382	69,344	41	182,268
1979	444	84,347	44	257,952
1980	502	98,954	49	312,206
1981	564	115,714	52	349,008
1982	631	143,690	56	392,992
1983	704	154,086	62	421,987
1984	783	175,185	67	465,956
1985	867	197,592	76	501,921
1986	951	223,383	80	580,077
1987	1,051	239,153	91	626,118
1988	1,141	256,868	98	700,975
1989	1,234	280,000	108	752,000

*Table does not include persons who accepted lump-sum settlements. The average benefit to beneficiaries of tax-qualified plans is much larger because these benefits are typically for a fixed period of time, while employees' pension fund benefits are more often life annuities.

SOURCE: Mitsubishi Trust and Banking Corporation, "Mitsubishi's Pension Bulletin," and Actuarial Department of Pension Fund Association, "Annual Report of EPF Services," as reported in Pension Fund Association, *Corporate Pension Plans in Japan* (Tokyo: 1989), p. 22. Data for 1989 are reported in Yoshiro Yumiba, "Private Pension Statistics in Japan," in *Pension Policy: An International Perspective*, ed. John Turner and Lorna Dailey (Washington, D.C.: U.S. Government Printing Office, forthcoming).

Both employees' pension funds and tax-qualified pensions can be voluntarily terminated under present governmental regulations. The rate of termination of tax-qualified pensions has been very high.[22] In the year ended March 31, 1988, 1,857 tax-qualified plans were terminated. This was 2.6 percent of the plans operating at the beginning of the year. By contrast, only 18 employees' pension funds have terminated since these plans were initiated in the late 1960s.

In 1989, a pension guaranty system was instituted only for employees' pension funds. This system is operated by the Pension Fund Association, an organization composed of the employees' pension funds. At present, there is no comparable program for tax-qualified pensions, and these are the plans most at risk of being terminated.

Both types of pension plans penalize quitting prior to retirement. The pension penalty for quitting is due to the relatively long vesting period and benefit formulas based on final earnings. This penalty for quitting is similar to that imposed on U.S. workers who are covered by defined benefit pension plans. In these plans, the formula used for workers who quit prior to retirement is typically the same as used for long-term employees who work until retirement. However, early quitters receive lower benefits because their pension is based on earnings when they left the firm, which are much lower than earnings at retirement would have been.[23] In both cases, reduction in retirement benefits can be expected to reduce turnover. These compensation systems are consistent with long-term employment contracts, which attempt to reduce labor costs by reducing turnover.[24]

Pension plans are funded based on projected earnings that reflect only seniority wage increases. Therefore, rising wages due to inflation and productivity continue to create unfunded liabilities, which must be funded along with new pension accruals. The reserve funds of both types of plans are subject to a tax; however, there is a high exemption for employees' pension funds, so most of these plans are not taxed.

The pension financial market is highly regulated. All funds must be invested with either a trust bank or an insurance company. The standard practice in the industry is to bundle all financial services together and to charge a single fee. The government has identified eight acceptable trust banks and 21 life insurance companies that are permitted to handle pension assets. Recently, nine additional foreign trust banks have been approved to manage pension funds. Approved banks include Bankers' Trust Company, Chase Manhattan Bank, Chemical Bank, Citibank, Manufacturers Hanover Trust, J. P. Morgan, Barclays Bank of London, Credit Suisse, and Union Bank of Switzerland. Together, these non-Japanese banks managed about 24.5 billion yen ($191 million at a first-quarter 1989 exchange rate of 128.5 yen per dollar) of pension assets, or about 1 percent of pension funds.[25]

Tables 5–10 and 5–11 indicate the composition of pension portfolios managed by trust banks and insurance companies. In 1987, pension assets managed by trust banks totaled 14.1 trillion yen ($97.5 billion at an exchange rate of 144.6 yen per dollar). All trust banks provide separate accounts for each pension plan. Investments can be tailored to the desires of each plan manager subject to approved investment practices. Both types of plans must meet the same limits on the composition of the investment portfolio. Government and other Japanese bonds composed 31 percent of the pension funds portfolio in 1987, while Japanese stocks represented 25 percent and foreign securities, 16 percent.

Pension assets managed by insurance companies are collectively invested with other assets of these companies. The composition of the total assets managed by insurance companies (including the pension

TABLE 5–10 Pension Fund Assets Managed by Trust Banks in Billion Yen*

	1985	1986	1987
Contributions to government investment and loans	1,436 (13.6)	1,574 (12.9)	1,311 (9.3)
Loans	1,710 (16.2)	1,857 (15.2)	1,987 (14.1)
Money credit trust	416 (3.9)	294 (2.4)	118 (0.8)
Government bonds	1,718 (16.2)	1,033 (8.5)	633 (4.5)
Other bonds	2,634 (24.9)	3,645 (29.9)	3,792 (26.9)
Personal estate trust	102 (1.0)	93 (0.8)	66 (0.5)
Stocks	1,340 (12.7)	1,951 (16.0)	3,469 (24.6)
Real estate trust	245 (2.3)	239 (2)	201 (1.4)
Real estate	35 (0.3)	77 (0.6)	115 (0.8)
Foreign securities	881 (8.3)	1,160 (9.5)	2,200 (15.6)
Others	63 (0.6)	287 (2.4)	216 (1.5)
Total	10,580 (100)	12,210 (100)	14,108 (100)

*Data are for March of each year. Values in parentheses are percent of total assets in the year.
SOURCE: Pension Fund Association, *Corporate Pension Plans in Japan* (Tokyo: 1987), p. 30.

assets) are shown in Table 5–11. Returns on investments are credited to each pension fund against a book value.[26]

David Crawford compared per capita pension assets in the United States and Japan. He estimated that on December 31, 1987, assets in private pension funds in Japan totaled $207 billion. With 59 million employed persons, this represented $3,508 per employee. Total pension plan assets in the United States were $1,460 billion, or $13,036 for each of 112 million employees. He concludes that "since corporate retirement benefit levels are broadly comparable in the two countries, the overall underfunding in Japan is striking." The underfunding of Japanese plans is attributed to the underrecognition of future retirement benefit costs due to funding that does not anticipate future wage increases. Crawford includes both pensions and lump-sum payment plans in his analysis.[27] As noted earlier, most lump-sum payment plans are not funded.

TABLE 5–11 Total Assets Managed by Insurance Companies in Billion Yen*

	1985	1986	1987
Savings	3,045	6,249	7,571
	(6.7)	(11.6)	(11.6)
Call loans	114	147	130
	(0.2)	(0.3)	(0.2)
Securities (total)	16,051	18,981	26,792
	(35.1)	(35.2)	(41.0)
Public corporation bonds	5,014	6,076	8,166
	(11.0)	(11.3)	(12.5)
Stocks	6,922	8,114	11,101
	(15.1)	(15.1)	(17.0)
Foreign securities	4,029	4,668	7,525
	(8.8)	(8.7)	(11.5)
Other securities	87	123	0
	(0.2)	(0.2)	(0)
Loans	23,064	24,372	25,637
	(50.4)	(45.2)	(39.2)
Real estate	2,741	3,196	3,777
	(6)	(5.9)	(5.8)
Others	726	926	1,411
	(1.6)	(1.7)	(2.2)
Total	45,740	53,871	65,318
	(100)	(100)	(100)

*Data are for March of each year. Values in parentheses are percent of total assets in the year. Pension fund assets managed by insurance companies are collectively invested with other assets.

SOURCE: Pension Fund Association, *Corporate Pension Plans in Japan* (Tokyo: 1987), p. 30.

Pensions are a relatively recent addition to labor compensation in Japan. Just as in the United States, firms are encouraged to adopt pension plans through tax incentives. If plans are adopted, they are highly regulated by the government. Tax-qualified plans appear to provide preferential tax treatment to firms while providing the traditional lump-sum retirement payment. This conclusion follows from the almost universal inclusion of lump-sum options in these plans and the high rate of selection of the lump-sum payments.

Employees' pension funds are directly linked to the earnings-related social security benefits. These plans privatize this component of social security for covered workers. The long-run implications for national savings and for the reserves of the Employees' Pension Insurance system are now being considered in Japan. To understand the Japanese retirement income system, one must consider employer pensions along with social security, lump-sum payments, and the nature of employment relationships, including mandatory retirement.

ENDNOTES

1. Hisako Inoue, "A Pension System in Japan," *Otemon Economic Studies,* 1980, pp. 1–27, reports that only 10 percent of tax-qualified pension plans offered life annuities, while 88 percent provided a fixed-term annuity of between 10 and 14 years.

2. Nippon Dantai Life Insurance Company, "Recent Studies on Severance and Retirement Benefit Plans," August 1988, p. 8.

3. Kiyoshi Murakami, "Post-Retirement Benefit Plans in Japan," *Japan Insurance News,* p. 20.

4. Arithmetic average yield to maturity of all government bonds with seven years to maturity. Monthly series are compiled from end-of-month prices quoted on the Tokyo Stock Exchange. See International Monetary Fund, *International Financial Statistics* (Washington, D.C.: October 1989).

5. The accumulated increase in consumer prices between 1982 and 1988 was only 8 percent.

6. Kiyoshi Murakami, "Retirement Benefits and Pension Plans in Japan," Sophia University Business Series no. 118, 1988, p. 16.

7. Shuichi Kubayashi, "Employees' Pension Funds," *Benefits and Compensation International,* April 1989, p. 6. Junichi Sakamoto of the Pension Bureau indicated that only 20 or so employees' pension funds actually paid any tax on fund assets.

8. The rate for females is scheduled to increase annually by .15 percent until the contribution rate for women equals that for men.

9. Pension Fund Association, *Corporate Pension Plans in Japan* (Tokyo: 1989), p. 34.

10. Katsuyuki Nonoshita and Junichi Sakamoto, "Introduction of the Pension Benefit Guaranty System in Japan," unpublished paper, August 1989, p. 9.

11. Shuichi Kobayashi, "Employees' Pension Funds," *Benefits and Compensation International,* April 1989, p. 7.

12. Ibid, p. 15.

13. IBIS, February 1989, p. 18.

14. Pension Fund Association, *Corporate Pension Plans in Japan* (Tokyo: 1989), p. 16. As of 1989, there were 109 certified pension actuaries in Japan.

15. Kobayashi, "Employees' Pension Funds," April 1989, p. 6.

16. Employees' Pension Fund Association, *Proposal of a Statutory System of Qualified Pension Actuary* (Tokyo: April 1986), p. 52.

17. Nonoshita and Sakamoto, "Introduction of the Pension Benefit Guaranty System in Japan," pp. 12–13.

18. Some large companies have both types of pension plans. Thus, some workers are covered by an employees' pension fund and a tax-qualified pension plan. This dual coverage implies that somewhat less than 57 percent of all participants in the Employees' Pension Insurance system are covered by at least one of these plans. Yoshiro Yumiba, "Private Pension Statistics in Japan," in *Pension Policy: An International Perspective*, ed. John Turner and Lorna Dailey (Washington, D.C.: U.S. Government Printing Office, forthcoming) estimates that 10 percent of active participants are covered by both plans.

19. Nonoshita and Sakamoto, "Introduction of the Pension Benefit Guaranty System in Japan," p. 21; and IBIS, March 1989, p. 29.

20. Murakami, "Post-Retirement Benefit Plans in Japan," p. 19.

21. Employees' Pension Fund Association, *Proposal of a Statutory System of Qualified Pension Actuary*, p. 7.

22. Nonoshita and Sakamoto, "Introduction of the Pension Benefit Guaranty System in Japan."

23. Richard Ippolito, "Why Federal Workers Don't Quit," *Journal of Human Resources*, Spring 1987, pp. 281–99; and Steven Allen, Robert Clark, and Ann McDermed, "Pension Cost of Changing Jobs," *Research on Aging*, December 1988, pp. 459–71.

24. Edward Lazear, "Why Is There Mandatory Retirement?" *Journal of Political Economy*, December 1979, pp. 1261–84.

25. Barry Burr, "Japanese Door Ajar," *Pension and Investment Age*, February 1989, p. 33.

26. Shoji Yamada, "Decision-Making Process," *Benefits and Compensation International*, April 1989, p. 9.

27. David Crawford, "The Impact of Aging and Cultural Changes on Pensions in Japan and Its Relationship to the U.S.", paper presented at the Employee Benefit Research Institute Policy Forum, "Aging in Japan: Lessons for the U.S.?" July 26, 1989, in Washington, D.C., p. 10.

CHAPTER 6

_____Lessons from the Japanese_____
_____Experience for_____
_____U.S. Pension Policy_____

The Japanese system of retirement plans includes both public and private systems. The social security system includes both the National Pension flat benefit with universal coverage and a system of earnings-related plans, of which Employees' Pension Insurance covers most workers. These plans were significantly amended in 1985 by altering the benefit formulas to lower projected costs. Even with these changes, contribution rates will rise sharply due to the aging of the population. As a result, the government is considering raising the age of eligibility for benefits and is encouraging firms to retain older workers.

The private pension system has grown substantially in the last two decades. Legislation in the 1960s established the framework for employees' pension funds and tax-qualified pension plans. These two types of pension plans have developed rapidly within the limits of government regulations. These plans, in conjunction with lump-sum retirement payments, form the basis of the private retirement system.

The retirement plans are integral parts of the Japanese industrial relations system, which includes seniority pay, long-term employment, and relatively young mandatory retirement. The aging of the labor force increases firm labor costs due to the seniority-based pay structure. Having more older workers also increases labor costs through increases in pension costs due to the link between pension benefits, years of service, and final earnings.

The problems raised by an aging population represent one of the major challenges facing the Japanese government and its social insurance programs. In addition, private firms must adjust to the shift from the young labor force of the 1970s and early 1980s to the rapidly aging labor force of the future. This report has outlined the evolution of retirement systems to date and identified the responses to population aging. Since the United States is confronting similar demographic changes, the Japanese experience provides useful insights into the effectiveness of alternative pension policies.

This study has yielded several important findings concerning Japanese retirement systems. First, the population of Japan is rapidly aging, and this is changing Japan from a relatively young nation to one of the oldest in the world in the span of three decades. These demographic changes have required the government and private industry to respond to an aging labor force. Although the United States faced the early stages of population aging a decade before Japan did, in the future Japan will confront the challenges of a mature, older population before the United States will. Thus, policymakers in the United States should examine the Japanese reaction to further population aging for insights into possible changes in public policies.

Second, one of the first challenges of population aging to confront developed countries has been the increase in cost of social security systems due to increases in the ratio of retirees to workers and a maturing pension system. Just as did the United States, Japan recently amended its social security system to reduce projected cost increases. The 1985 social security reforms sharply reduced the benefit formula. This action was aimed at maintaining the gross replacement ratio at approximately 70 percent for married workers with nonworking spouses. Without these changes, the gross replacement rate for married retirees with nonworking spouses would have risen to about 83 percent.

The Diet is now considering proposals to raise the age of eligibility for benefits. These actions parallel policy initiatives in the United States enacted in 1977 and 1983. However, these changes are opposite of the European experience, where governments have encouraged early retirements as a policy to counteract relatively high rates of unemployment.[1]

Third, in an effort to provide a greater component of retirement income from private sources, the Japanese government has encouraged the adoption of private pensions. Preferential tax treatment for funded pensions was introduced in the 1960s. In the subsequent two decades, pensions have spread through the private sector.

Coverage rates by private retirement programs approach 90 percent in Japan, compared to around 50 percent in the United States.

Much of this difference is due to coverage by lump-sum severance payments, which are the traditional method of retirement payments in Japan. Annuity pension plans in Japan cover 58 percent of workers who are participating in the employee component of social security, the Employees' Pension Insurance system.

Fourth, several aspects of the employees' pension funds and tax-qualified pension plans provide useful insights for pension policy in the United States. Recently, attention in the United States has focused on whether lump-sum distributions should be permitted. In Japan, most plans have lump-sum options. Virtually all participants in tax-qualified pension plans and half of the employees' pension fund participants select lump-sum options. The popularity of these options may be due to the traditional lump-sum payment systems; however, their widespread use suggests how retirees in the United States may behave if given the option of lump-sum distributions.

Just as in the United States, Japanese private pensions are not required to provide inflation increases, and few—if any—plans automatically award such increases. Available information indicates that few pension plans provide ad hoc increases. This differs from the U.S. experience, where large employers have been found to provide regular ad hoc benefit increases. However, these increases are typically less than the rate of inflation.

Periodically, there have been proposals to privatize part of the U.S. social security system. In Japan, employees' pension funds have contracted out the earnings component of social security. The employees' pension funds are required to create a reserve fund, and the government regulates these investments. Proponents of privatizing social security should study the Japanese system, which has developed over the last two decades. The effect of the employees' pension fund system on national savings is a topic that needs further study and may provide useful information on the differential effects of unfunded social security in comparison to a private, funded system, which takes the place of a portion of social security.

An additional aspect of the employees' pension fund system that merits further attention is the use of the Pension Fund Association as a portability center for workers who move across firms with employees' pension funds. The portability applies only to the contracted-out benefit. Advocates of greater portability among pensions in the United States may wish to examine the performance of the Pension Fund Association in providing benefits to workers who leave an employees' pension fund prior to retirement. This may be a manageable job, because relatively few workers move among employers with employees' pension funds.

Tax-qualified plans are audited at least every five years, and excess funds must be returned to the employer. At no other time can funds be withdrawn. The remaining assets are viewed as belonging to the participants. At the termination of a plan, the assets are divided among the participants. This system, along with strict full-funding limits, precludes the use of plan assets in firm takeovers. Employees' pension funds are also subject to regular governmental review; however, excess assets in these plans must remain in the fund.

Several other differences in pension policy are worth emphasizing. Japan has no system of defined contribution plans. Currently, there is some discussion of permitting the adoption of a voluntary defined contribution plan for self-employed workers, who are covered only by the National Pension component of social security.[2]

In contrast to U.S. policy, pension fund assets are taxed by the Japanese government at the rate of 1 percent per year plus a small local tax. Exemptions to these taxes result in most employees' pension funds having only limited tax liabilities.

In an effort to delay withdrawal from the labor force, the Japanese government is offering subsidies to firms that hire older workers. The Japanese government has outlined goals and objectives for the continuation of work. No statistical studies have attempted to estimate the effectiveness of these policies. It is clear, however, that the labor force participation rates of older men are much higher than they are in other developed countries, and these rates have declined less rapidly than those in the European countries or in the United States.

Another aspect of the Japanese labor market that varies greatly from the United States is the system of reemployment after mandatory retirement. Reemployed workers lose their seniority status, are paid lower wages, and do not receive seniority-based wage increases. Such policies would clearly be illegal under U.S. age discrimination laws.

Sixth, among developed countries, Japan has the highest labor force participation rates for older persons. These high rates prevail despite the widespread use of mandatory retirement policies by many companies. In recent years, firms have raised the age of mandatory retirement from approximately 55 toward age 60. Government policy is to have mandatory retirement at age 60 or higher, but firms are not required to comply.

In summary, several aspects of Japanese pensions are directly related to current pension policy debates in the United States. Changes in government policies concerning the employment of older workers and social security in response to the continuing aging of the population also will be of interest. Greater knowledge concerning these concepts in Japan may provide useful information to U.S. policymakers.

ENDNOTES

1. Barry Mirkin, "Early Retirement as a Labor Force Policy: An International Overview," *Monthly Labor Review*, March 1987, pp. 19–33.
2. Kiyoshi Murakami, "Aging and Pensions in Japan," paper presented at the Employee Benefit Research Institute Policy Forum, "Aging in Japan: Lessons from the U.S.?" p. 5.

Index

Age Discrimination in Employment Act (U.S., 1967), 16, 19
Aging population, 3–10
  compared to other industrial countries, 5
  population ratios compared to United States, 6
  problems for pension plans, 7–10, 94–95
Agricultural, Forestry and Fishery Institutions Employees' Mutual Aid Association, 3, 27, 29
Allen, Steven, 93
Andrews, Emily, 67
Anker, Richard, 11, 22, 25, 26
Annuity pension plans, 52, 55, 70–72, 96

Bankers' Trust Company, 89
Barclays Bank of London, 89
Barker, David, 25
Bednarzik, R. W., 25
Birth and death rates, 5, 8
Blinder, Alan, 50
Bonuses, 12
Book reserve, 63, 64
Burkhauser, Richard, 25
Burr, Barry, 93
Burtless, Gary, 51

Canada, projection of pension expenditures, 10

Capital gains taxation, 54
Chase Manhattan Bank, 89
Chemical Bank, 89
Citibank, 89
Clark, Robert, 11, 22, 25, 26, 93
Cole, Robert, 24
Corporate income taxes, 57–58
Cowper, C. C., 25
Crawford, David, 90, 93
Credit Suisse, 89

Dailey, Lorna, 17, 67, 86, 88, 93
Defined contribution plans, 97
Dore, Ronald, 24
Durand, John, 11

Employee Retirement Income Security Act (ERISA) (U.S.), 62
Employees' pension funds, 2–3, 69, 74–84
  benefit determination, 76–78
  compared to tax-qualified pensions, 85–91
  distribution of funds, 75–76
  pension guaranty system, 88
  plan funding and administration, 79–81
  termination of funds, 81–84
  vesting of benefits, 78–79

Employees' Pension Insurance Law
  (1965), 74
Employees' Pension Insurance program,
  1–3, 22–23, 27, 29, 38–46, 48, 85, 94
  adjustment for inflation, 48
  benefit determination, 39–44
  contribution rates, 30–31
  costs, 30–31
  financing, 45–46
  implications for national savings, 91
  income replacement, 48
  reserves, 31–32, 33–34
  retirement age and earnings test,
    44–45
  tax rate, 46
Employment, 12
  government policies, 19–21
  job tenure, 12
  long-term, 12, 14
  part-time, 12–13
  after retirement, 17–19, 22
  self-employment, 2–3, 28, 33–35
  seniority, 13
  women, 12–13
Employment Promotion Measures Act
  (1966), 20
Ernsberger, Nicole, 49, 50

France
  costs of public pension plans, 9–10
  rate of population aging, 5
  social security system, 27
Fujita, Yoshitaka, 24, 25, 67, 68
Fukao, Mitsuhiro, 49

Germany
  projection of pension expenditures, 10
  rate of population aging, 5
  social security programs, 27
Gordon, Roger, 50
Guralnik, Jack, 11

Hashimoto, K., 67
Hashimoto, Nasanori, 24
Heller, Peter, 11
Hemming, Richard, 10
Homma, H., 67
Hoshimo, Shinya, 26

Iliromitsu, Ishi, 11
Industrial relations system, 3, 13–14
Inoue, Hisaka, 92
Insurance companies, 89–90, 91
Ippolito, Richard, 93
Italy
  projection of pension expenditures, 10
  social security system, 27

Jones, Randall, 49
J. P. Morgan Company, 89

Kaizuka, Keimei, 67
Kii, Toshi, 25
Kobayashi, Shuichi, 92
Kohnert, Peter, 10
Kotlikoff, Laurence, 50, 51
Kubayashi, Shuichi, 92

Labor force
  aging, 3–5, 7
  job tenure, 12
  participation rates, 3, 21–23
  part-time workers, 12–13
  women, 12–13
Labor markets, 12–14
Lazear, Edward, 93
Life expectancy, 5, 9
Liu, Lillian, 33, 49
Local Public Service Mutual Aid Association, 3, 27, 29
Lump-sum retirement payment, 1–3, 7–
  8, 52, 55, 59–66, 96
  calculation of benefits, 62–63
  changing nature of, 65–66
  private pension funds, 69–72, 87
  qualifying for benefits, 61, 62
  reserve funding, 63–64
  Small Enterprise Retirement Allow-
    ance Mutual Aid Plan, 64–65

McCallum, John, 26
McDermid, Ann, 93
Maeda, T., 67
Mandatory retirement, 3, 13, 14–17
  distribution of ages, 16–17
  government policy, 15–16
  reemployment, 97

Manufacturers Hanover Trust, 89
Marginal tax rates, 56
Markides, K. S., 25
Martin, Linda, 11
Merit pay systems, 13
Mirkin, Barry, 98
Moffitt, Robert, 51
Munnell, Alicia, 49, 50
Murakami, Hiroshi, 50
Murakami, Kiyoshi, 17, 44, 50, 61, 62, 67, 68, 74, 92, 93, 98

Nagono, Atushi, 55–67
National Mutual Insurance Federation of Agricultural Cooperatives (Zenky-oren), 73–74
National Pension Plan, 1–3, 22–23, 27–31, 34–38, 48, 94
benefit determination, 36
benefit payments, 44
contributions, 32
costs, 31
financing, 34–36
insurable period, 38
reserves, 33
retirement penalties and credits, 37
National Public Service Mutual Aid Association, 3, 27, 29
Noguchi, Yukio, 49
Nonoshita, Katsuyuki, 82, 84, 92, 93

Ogawa, Maohiro, 11, 12
Organization for Economic Cooperation and Development (OECD), 53
Osako, Masako, 25

Part-time employees, 12–13
Patrick, Hugh, 67
Pechman, Joseph, 67
Pension actuary, 80
Pension financial market, 89
insurance companies, 89–91
trust banks, 89–90
Pension Fund Association, 79, 81–84, 87–88, 96
Pension guaranty system, 88
Pension Insurance Amendments (1985), 28
objectives, 28

Pension plans, 1–2, 9, 52; see also Employees' Pension Insurance program and National Pension Plan
annuities, 52, 55–56, 70–72, 96
expenditure rates, 9–10
lessons for United States from Japanese pension experience, 94–97
lump sum; see Lump-sum retirement payment
private sector; see Private pension plans
tax policies affecting, 58–59
Population aging; see Aging population
Premium Payment Guaranty Project Steering Committee, 83
Private pension plans, 2–3, 69–91, 94–96
employees' pension funds, 69, 74–84
inflation increases, 96
lump-sum retirement payments, 69–72, 87
nonqualified, 84–85
per capita pension assets, 90
tax-qualified pensions, 69–74
Private School Teachers and Employees' Mutual Aid Association, 3, 27, 29
Public workers' retirement plans, 2
costs, 9

Quinn, Joseph, 25
Raisian, John, 24
Reemployment, 19, 22, 97
Retirement
age, 44
earnings test, 44–45
mandatory; see Mandatory retirement
policies for an aging society, 23–24
tax policies affecting income, 52–59
work after retirement, 17–19
earnings reduction, 22
Retirement payment plans
annuity pension fund; see Annuity pension plans
lump sum; see Lump-sum retirement payment
Rosovsky, Henry, 67

Sakamoto, Junichi, 68, 82, 84, 92, 93
Sakuma, Ken, 26
Satoshi, Kamata, 26
Seike, Atsushi, 51
Self-employed workers, 1–3

Seniority-based pay systems, 13, 15, 23
Severance pay, 52
  lump sum; see Lump-sum retirement
    payment
Shields, C. R., 25
Shimada, Haruo, 24, 25, 68
Shoven, John, 50, 56, 66, 67
Silver talent or manpower centers, 20–21
Small Enterprise Retirement Allowance
    Mutual Aid Plan, 64–65
Small Saving Tax Exemption, 54
Social security system, 1, 27; see also
    Employees' Pension Insurance pro-
    gram and National Pension Plan
  cost increases, 30–38
  problems and prospects, 46–48
  replacement ratio, 46–47
  statutory pension schemes, 29
  women, 28, 47
Social Security Trust Fund reserves, 33
Special Retirement Allowance Mutual
    Aid Plan, 64
Spengler, Joseph, 11
Stabilization of Employment for Elderly
    Persons Act (1986), 16
Statutory pension schemes, 29
Sweden, social security system, 27
System for Savings for the Formation of
    Employees' Assets, 54, 55

Tachibanaki, Toskiaki, 50
Takada, Kazuo, 25, 26
Takeuchi, Kunio, 50
Talent Banks, 20
Tax policy, 52–59
  capital gains, 54
  corporate income tax, 57–58
  growth of pension funds, 58–59
  marginal tax rates, 56
  overall tax burden as percent of
    GNP, 53
  pension fund assets, 97
  personal income taxation, 53–57
  retirement income, 52
  savings, 54
Tax-qualified pension plans, 2, 69–70
  auditing, 97
  benefit determination, 70
  compared to employees' pension
    funds, 85–91
  financing of, 72

Tax-qualified pension plans—*Cont.*
  growth of coverage, 73–74
  preferential tax treatment, 91
  tax status of benefits, 71
Toda, Shunichiro, 50
Trust banks, 89, 90
Trust Fund Bureau of Ministry of
    Finance, 33
Turner, John, 17, 67, 86, 88, 93

Union Bank of Switzerland, 89
United Kingdom
  public pension plan costs, 9–10
  rate of population aging, 5
  social security system, 27
United States
  age-specific labor force participation,
    21, 22
  cost of public pension plans, 9–10
  earnings test, 45
  lessons from Japanese experience for
    U.S. pension plans, 94–97
  mandatory retirement policy, 16
  overall tax burden as percent of
    GNP, 53
  per capita pension assets, 90
  population ratios, 6
  rate of population aging, 5
  retirement tax system compared to
    Japan, 10
  social security system, 96
West Germany
  projection of pension expenditures, 10
  rate of population aging, 5
Wise, Donald, 50
Women
  employment, 12–13
  labor force participation rates, 21–23
  pensionable age, 44
  earnings, 12
  social security system, 28, 47

Yamada, Shoji, 93
Yamada, Tadashi, 50
Yamada, Tetsuji, 50
Yanagishita, Michiko, 11
Yujta, Yoshitaka, 50
Yumiba, Yoshiro, 86, 93

Zenkyoren (National Mutual Insurance
    Federation of Agricultural Coopera-
    tives), 73–74